The Real Rosebud

The Real Rosebud

The Triumph of a Lakota Woman

MARJORIE WEINBERG

Foreword by Luke Yellow Robe

University of Nebraska Press, Lincoln and London

© 2004 by the
Board of Regents
of the University
of Nebraska
Foreword © 2004 by
Luke Yellow Robe
All rights reserved
Manufactured in the
United States of
America ⊗
Library of Congress
Cataloging-in-
Publication Data
Weinberg, Marjorie,
1934–
The real Rosebud :
the triumph of a
Lakota woman /
Marjorie Weinberg ;
foreword by Luke
Yellow Robe.   p. cm.
Includes biblio-
graphical references
and index.
ISBN 0-8032-4803-3
(cl.: alk. paper)
1. Yellow Robe,
Rosebud.   2. Teton
women – New York
(State) – New York –
Biography.   3. Teton
women – New York
(State) – Jones Beach
State Park – Biogra-
phy.   4. Teton
Indians – Social life
and customs.   I. Title.
E99.T34 Y448 2004
974.7'2450049752
– dc21   2003012755

This book is dedicated with love
to the memory of my teacher,
friend, and second mother,
ROSEBUD YELLOW ROBE

Contents

ILLUSTRATIONS

following page 44

Foreword

We are a sum total of what we have learned from all who have taught us, both great and small. I'm grateful for the inspiration and wisdom of my grandmother, Rosebud Yellow Robe. Grandma Rosebud set in motion for her people and family a lifetime pursuit of achievement and learning, a pursuit to be duplicated so that we can see the importance of rising above circumstance. Her example has served as an internal compass that has inspired me to navigate through the obstacles and barriers of life in order to be an inspiration. Her pursuits have served as blueprints of what can be accomplished interdependently for the good of all Native people and all people who aspire to make contributions in many forms to society.

The experts say we are all products of our environments. By her commitment and dedication to becoming the best she could be, I'm inspired to do the same. Grandma Rosebud has fashioned the lenses of how we see our world around us by creating examples for her family to follow, and for this we will be forever grateful.

For the development and production of this book itself, I feel a deep sense of gratitude to Marjorie Weinberg. She and Grandma together have achieved a lifetime of memories to be shared by all. Marjorie, your friendship and love for Rosebud, along with countless hours of research and dedication, have brought *The Real Rosebud* to fruition. From the depths of our hearts we thank you, as our children's children will know about the generations of family who helped establish their foundation of growth.

In grateful acknowledgment,

Luke Yellow Robe, Rosebud's grandson
Cultural Relations Director, Children's Home Society of South Dakota

Preface

The Real Rosebud

For as long as I can remember, Rosebud would answer the inevitable question "Were you named after the sled?" with "Why no, the sled was named after me." In fact, Rosebud was named by her father, Chauncey Yellow Robe, for the Rosebud Reservation in South Dakota, where her Lakota (Teton Sioux) family was enrolled, although she was born in Rapid City, South Dakota.

Orson Welles's film classic *Citizen Kane* ends with the word "Rosebud," the name of Kane's sled, symbolizing the happy times of his childhood, the one thing he longs for on his deathbed. Welles never revealed the source of the name "Rosebud." His biographer, David Thomson, suggests that even though the sled may seem to be a "hokey device," in the context of the movie it "works wonderfully well."[1] But he was unaware that a real Rosebud existed.

In 1991, Ed Castle, a reporter for the *Las Vegas Sun*, was sure he had discovered the inspiration for "Rosebud."[2] In a pair of articles that delighted Rosebud Yellow Robe, Castle determined that the daily sign-in sheets at CBS held the answer to the puzzle. During the 1930s both Rosebud and Orson Welles were broadcasting radio shows from the CBS studios in New York. Rosebud hosted a children's program called *Aunt Susan*, recounting Indian legends and stories learned from her father. Orson Welles's *Mercury Theatre on the Air* became famous in 1938 when his broadcast of *The War of the Worlds*, an altogether too lifelike report of a Martian invasion, caused panic among radio audiences across the country.

At CBS each radio actor signed the daily log on arriving and on leaving the studio. Rosebud's signature appears in these logs on the same pages as

Welles's, and although they were not acquainted, they must have seen each other in the studio. Moreover, Rosebud bore a remarkable resemblance to the actress Dolores Del Rio, whom Welles loved; in fact, Cecil B. DeMille first offered Rosebud the title role later played by Del Rio in the 1928 film *Ramona*. By naming the sled "Rosebud," could Welles have linked Kane's symbol of happiness to his own happiness with Del Rio?

Together, the CBS logs and the connection with Dolores Del Rio were proof enough for Rosebud's many friends that Welles's "Rosebud" was "our" Rosebud.

Acknowledgments

In the more than forty years it has taken to complete *The Real Rosebud*, many remarkable people have given of themselves in many different ways to the "cause." First was Rosebud herself, who wanted her family's story told and until her death actively participated in the research and encouraged me to continue. She so delightfully entangled me in the quest for knowledge of her family that it became a primary goal of my own.

I am grateful to my parents for encouraging my friendship with Rosebud, and to my late sister, Roberta, who not only tagged along but also became a loving friend to Rosebud. My late husband, Hy, enabled me to undertake graduate work in anthropology and to pursue this journey. At New York University I had the singular good fortune to meet and study with Karen Blu; time and again she introduced me to scholars, later to become friends, who showed me the way to final publication. Through her recommendation I asked Joan Lehn, one of Karen's former students, to help me with editing. That was five and a half years ago. During these years, Joan has become a dear friend, a sturdy traveler, and a most knowledgeable adviser. Also at NYU I met and married Paul Berman, who has supported this project throughout our South Dakota travels and on the many other roads it has taken me.

My children, Joyce, Bruce, and Robert, who grew up knowing Rosebud and greatly admired her, gave me their loving help along the way. My nieces, Alison and Karen, also encouraged my endeavors. Evelyn Finkbeiner, Karen and Taki Moy, Al Frantz, and Mary, Luke, Deb, Glen, Rose, Alice, Sophia, and the rest of the Yellow Robe family all offered me more than friendship. They gave me their own versions of stories passed down through the generations. Other members of Rosebud's family – Chauncina's daughter, Fawn Sitman; Shirley Plume and her daughters – showed interest in the developing story. Ed Morrow kindly shared his memories of Rosebud, his fellow student at the University of South Dakota. Ann Achee and Ike Kantor proved to be steadfast friends to the Yellow Robes and to me.

Within this last year, Dr. Blu introduced me to another friend and special fellow scholar, Ray DeMallie, who took the manuscript and me under his wing. Gary Dunham, on Dr. DeMallie's recommendation, supported the book for publication.

So many people helped along the route of my travels, everyone adding yet another crucial bit, that I can hardly hope to name them all here. Rosebud's and Evelyn's friends Betty Clark Rosenthal and Katherine Weiss, now dear friends of mine, were generous with their stories and support. Barbara Landis, Carlisle Indian School historian and Cumberland County Historical Society archivist, became an enthusiastic contributor along the way. When it was my good fortune to work as a volunteer at the Smithsonian Institution in Washington DC under the direction of JoAllyn Archambault and Christina Burke, they added their academic expertise.

During our time together as board members of Adelphi University, Jill Ker Conway, past president of Smith College and noted author, offered me her ear and was among the first to listen to the early chapters of my manuscript. It was she who advised me that I had a place in the story, too, thus making this family chronicle a story of mentoring and friendship as well.

LaVera Rose, state archivist at Pierre, South Dakota, guided me through the state archives, and Marcella Cash of Sinte Gleska University in Rosebud, South Dakota, helped in my research. Through Rosebud's connection with the University of South Dakota, I met and developed a friendship with Emogene Paulson and the late General Lloyd Moses. Ruth Ziolkowski, director of the Crazy Horse Monument in South Dakota, located materials in her archives concerning Chauncey Yellow Robe. The librarians in Rapid City and at the University of South Dakota were most helpful in locating information about the Yellow Robes, as was the staff at the W. H. Over Museum. Former archivist Karen Zimmerman, Christina Salem, and Dwight Hansen of the Development Office at the University of South Dakota all aided in my quest and were generous in sharing old photos. Rosebud put me in touch with Donald Smith, the biographer of Chief Buffalo Child/Long Lance; he provided material about *The Silent Enemy*, the film in which both Chauncey and Long Lance appeared.

William Hughes of Rapid City and the late Sidney Margolis of Santa Fe, New Mexico, sent much-needed books, and Lea Armstrong of the Wheelwright Museum of Santa Fe sent a remarkably timely reference.

At Jones Beach State Park, Frank Kollar and his secretary, Peggy Kucija, were instrumental in helping me to revive Rosebud's part in the history of Jones Beach, and the New York State Parks Department archives at Bethpage State Park yielded useful information.

Rosebud shared her friends as well as her family with me, including Helen Hill Wrede, Dorothy Hale, Pearl Hoel, all originally from Rapid City. Todd Berks, Suzanne Bloom, Esther Friedman, Irene Haas, Diane Kaufman, Brenda Lurin, Janet Marks, Ann McCoy, Barbara Paltrow, Jackie Roberts, Trudi Shepard, and Ruth Trattler were members of "the Birthday Club," which met annually on February 26 to celebrate Rosebud's birthday. Esther Friedman's daughters, Nancy Joseph and Sandy Nachbar, were auxiliary members, as were Robert Berks, Steven Haas, the late Richard Shepard, and Amy Spaulding.

Most of the people who appear in this long list have remained my friends. Many thanks also to those who helped in this journey but whose names may not be listed: please forgive the omissions and accept my gratitude.

The Real Rosebud

Introduction

Making the Promise

It started with that first marvelous summer of 1947 spent mostly at the Jones Beach Indian Village, where Rosebud Yellow Robe was the director. My own interest in Rosebud, her family, and her people – the Lakotas or Teton Sioux – developed immediately. On her father's side, Rosebud was a Lakota Indian, a member of the Brule tribe, who live on the Rosebud Reservation in South Dakota. Her grandfather on her father's side was Yellow Robe, a chief who fought against Lt. Col. George A. Custer and the Seventh Cavalry in the Battle of the Little Bighorn, and who was a relative of Sitting Bull.[1] Her father, Chauncey Yellow Robe, was widely admired as a successful graduate of the Carlisle Indian School in Pennsylvania and served as a bridge between the two worlds of the white majority and the Indian minority. He was proud of his accomplishments in both worlds. Her mother, Lillie Springer, who was of Swiss-German heritage, was born in the United States. She met Chauncey and they fell in love the year she volunteered to work as a nurse among the Indians of South Dakota. Together, they taught Rosebud to take pride in the best of both worlds.

Raised in South Dakota, Rosebud came to New York City in 1927, at the age of twenty, having spent the previous two years as a student at the University of South Dakota. For the remainder of her life, some sixty-five years, she made New York her home. College-educated Native women, proud of their heritage and culture and able to communicate that pride, were rare. Only a very few come to mind. Ella Deloria, Yankton Sioux, graduated from Columbia University Teachers' College and later collaborated with Franz Boas to write the definitive grammar of Lakota, the Sioux Indian language; she was also a popular lecturer on Indian culture and Indian causes, her presentations sponsored by the YWCA and church groups.[2] Te Ata (Mary Thompson) Fisher, Chickasaw-Choctaw, was a professional actress who appeared on Broadway and married Clyde Fisher, an astronomer at the American Museum of Natural History.[3] Ruth Muskrat Bronson, Cherokee, who began her career as a teacher at Haskell Institute in Lawrence, Kansas (one of the first Indian Schools), later held positions in the Bureau of Indian Affairs, where she was in charge of loans and scholarships for Indian college students.[4] Throughout her life, Rosebud Yellow Robe was prominent among these American Indian spokeswomen.

Rosebud came to New York long before television, in the age of radio and silent movies. Both offered only distorted stereotypes of Native culture. Easterners knew little about the actual lifeways of Indians. The fictional literature generally portrayed Indians as savages – either noble or cutthroat. All of Rosebud's activities in New York were aimed at educating the public about Native peoples. During the summers from 1930 to 1950 she directed the Jones Beach Indian Village. During the winters, dressed in tribal costume, Rosebud visited schools to tell stories. She said that when she first was introduced to schoolchildren in New York City, some were frightened and tried to hide under their desks. She told Sioux legends she had heard from her father, as well as stories from the Eastern Woodland tribes.

Rosebud was a feminine feminist, an attractive and talented communicator. When performing, she wore Native dress because it was an effective visual symbol of Indianness. With quiet dignity she was able to convey her pride in Lakota ways to audiences who otherwise knew nothing about American Indians.

Although this book concerns the history of an accomplished American Indian family, it is no less a story about mentoring. The true significance of Rosebud's guiding friendship to a floundering adolescent continues to unfold to this day. What I learned from her had much more to do with encouraging human relationships than with "Indianness." Her acceptance of people as they are, her responsiveness to the needs of others, and her ability to encourage their differences while rejoicing in their achievements still affect me as I approach my older years. She set forth ideals that serve as an example of what it means to be human and caring. She showed me that in a full life one needs to contribute positively to the lives of others. Although the purpose of this book is to tell the important story of Rosebud and the Yellow Robe family, it is also about a young girl who was lucky enough to find an adult willing and able to share herself. This good fortune enabled the emerging young woman to emulate an exceptional person.

When I was thirteen, my family moved from the familiar landmarks of Bay Ridge, Brooklyn, to the unknown streets of Queens Village, Queens. Bay Ridge was a bustling commercial area with a lovely waterfront; Queens Village was inland, a quiet suburban community. To me, the only similarities were the language and the currency. Everything else was new, different, and unmapped.

My father, a dentist whose office was connected to our Brooklyn apartment, had always been nearby. But after we moved, he had to drive back to Brooklyn a few days a week to keep his practice going there while he began a new one in Queens. My mother had been ill and could barely cope with the changes herself, let alone help an adolescent find her way. Our roles were reversed: I became my mother's mother, but where was someone to show me the way to a successful adulthood? Somehow for a time that first summer we managed without much structure, without school or camp. Then my father, realizing just how difficult the weeks had become, suggested that I write for information about the surrounding recreational programs available; he said he would drive my younger sister, Roberta, and me several days a week. Among the brochures that started arriving, the pamphlet announcing the activities at Jones Beach State Park sounded intriguing. As I told Dad, "It's really not too far, and look, it has everything."

On a promising day, a Friday, in mid-July 1947 we packed a lunch and took along an old army blanket and some chairs. After we settled ourselves on our beach turf, the rented umbrella in place, the blanket made secure against the wind with picnic basket, sand pail, books, and beach attire, I asked if I could explore the boardwalk. Being the older of two, usually dependable and responsible, I agreed on a time to return for lunch and was on my way. My younger sister wanted to play in the sand, so I was free to explore on my own. After walking just a few steps, I could not believe my eyes: right in front of me were three tipis positioned on the lawn near the boardwalk.

I could not have known then that Jones Beach was about to offer me, in the person of Rosebud Yellow Robe, a teacher, storyteller, artisan, and, most of all, an open and reachable adult. She was accepting of all who were willing to learn from her. To her close friends and family she gave unconditional love, and eventually, she would be there to understand and guide me. Each child received her rapt and undivided attention for as long as time permitted. She talked "up" to children and they responded by giving their best in all activities.

That first summer, my father drove my sister and me to the beach every Wednesday, Friday, Saturday, and Sunday. I soon became one of the regulars and was involved in many of the activities. When I wasn't at the beach, I was at the library reading everything I could find about American Indians. Only when the summer ended and the Indian Village closed for the winter did I realize how totally involved I had become in my studies, concentrating on the Lakotas. In my enthusiasm I even wrote to the Bureau of Indian Affairs requesting information about the Yellow Robes. A kindly clerk sent me a transcript of an obituary of Chauncey Yellow Robe that had originally appeared in a South Dakota newspaper.[5]

My family and I continued to spend many days each week at Jones Beach during the following summers. As Director of the Jones Beach Indian Village, Rosebud asked everyone simply to address her as "Rosebud," rather than as "Princess Rosebud" or "Miss Yellow Robe." She dressed in a nineteenth-century Lakota Indian costume: a deerskin dress, leggings, and moccasins, plus a feathered warbonnet (not customarily worn by women),[6] perhaps to protect her face from the sun. Sitting in front of the tipis, Rosebud would tell stories to an audience of children and adults, sing Indian songs, direct Indian games, and instruct all in Indian handicrafts – beadwork, basketry, and the making of warbonnets. She was never critical. "There are no problems," she said, "only solutions."

To become a participant in the Indian Village, all one had to do was to fill out an information card giving name, address, telephone number, and birth date for the use of the Long Island Park Commission. I had no idea that just writing my birth date would take on such extraordinary significance. Only later did Rosebud tell me that I was born the day and month on which both her mother and father had died, years before and three years apart. She added, "I always believed that they sent you to me to brighten my days." The fact that on Rosebud's sixty-first birthday I gave birth to identical twin sons served only to strengthen the importance of shared dates.

Evelyn Robe, Rosebud's sister, was on the faculty of Vassar College as I prepared for college and a career. She taught Speech Correction (now called Speech Pathology) and later earned her M.S. and Ph.D. at Northwestern University. She influenced my decision to pursue a career in speech pathology, for without her I would never have known of the profession that I have enjoyed my entire life.

During my college years at the University of Michigan I kept in occasional touch with Rosebud. After my marriage, a year in Philadelphia, and my return to Queens, we started an adult friendship that lasted until her death in 1992. During those years we shared ideas and hopes.

Rosebud longed to know more about her family, and for years she collected documents in preparation for writing a book about them. She enlisted me in her family history project, and since then, the quest for the story of Rosebud's ancestors on both sides of the Atlantic has fascinated me for more than fifty years. The journey into the past has taken on a life of its own and often resembles a treasure hunt. It has led me to travel to places that in the ordinary course of my life I would never have known about.

In 1983 I decided to enroll in graduate school. Although I had taken only a single course in anthropology at the University of Michigan, it seemed to me that the study of anthropology would provide the academic foundation to study and write the story of the Yellow Robe family. Consequently, I spent three years at New York University, where I wrote a master's thesis on the social impact of the development of Jones Beach, focusing on the Indian Village that Rosebud had created.[7] Much of that thesis is incorporated in this work.

In 1992, reflecting on her long life, Rosebud wrote, "My parents were the inspiration for what I have achieved. They learned to live in two worlds, Sioux and White, and won the respect of both. I still have to write their story. I hope to do so."[8] As she lay dying that year, I promised to complete the project for her.

Many of the stories in these pages were told to me by Rosebud during our years of research. We spent hours and days discussing her family's history, and this book is based on her memories as she passed them on to me over the long course of our friendship. I have relied on her recollections, first and foremost, as well as on other material she collected or preserved as family memorabilia, supplemented by my own academic research. Archival materials crucial to this work include the personal correspondence of Chauncey Yellow Robe and Lillian Springer Yellow Robe, and an unpublished biographical sketch of Chauncey Yellow Robe written by Ruth Brown in 1929 on the basis of interviews with him, a copy of which Rosebud provided me.

This memoir of Rosebud Yellow Robe and her family contributes in a personalized way to our understanding of how drastic change has affected the Native peoples of the United States over the past two centuries. I have used a wide range of sources to render the decisions made by individuals in the past more humanly understandable. It is easy to criticize, even to condemn, people of the past for actions and attitudes that are unpopular today, but politically correct revisionist history is not my goal. Throughout, I have tried to put the events of the past into the context of the Yellow Robes' time.

I

White Thunder to Yellow Robe

Rosebud never knew her grandfather, Yellow Robe (Thašína-ǧi), a chief of the Brule tribe of Lakotas. All that she knew of him came from her father's stories, but she was proud that her grandfather was known for his courage, vision, and leadership.

The Brule (Sichą́ǧu, "burned thigh") received their name at a time when they were camped on the shore of one of the long narrow lakes that are a feature of the country in eastern South Dakota. In a prairie grass fire about 1762–63, a man, his wife, and some children were burned to death; the rest of the people saved themselves by leaping into the lake, but most of them had their legs and thighs badly burned, and ugly scars resulted. Consequently, the French traders termed them *brulé*.[1] Yellow Robe was born during 1826–27, according to Swift Bear's winter count, a pictographic calendar painted on buffalo hide.[2] He was the son of Stabber (Wacháphe), a prominent Brule chief. His boyhood name was White Thunder, but he took the name of Yellow Robe in commemoration of his brave deed as a young man in a battle against the Crow Indians, hereditary enemies of the Lakotas.

The Yellow Robe family preserved a number of versions of this event, which vary in details. It must have occurred during the 1850s or early 1860s, when both the Crows and the Lakotas hunted along the tributaries of the Yellowstone River in what is now southern Montana. This region was one of the last places where the two tribes could still hunt buffalo, their economic mainstay.

In the story as told by Chauncey Yellow Robe, a Brule hunting party encountered a large Crow war party that was returning from a raid on a Lakota camp and had taken about twenty of the Lakotas' horses. The Crow leader, named Yellow Robe, was accompanied by his ten-year-old son. The boy was the old chief's greatest pride, so while the fight raged furiously about him, Yellow Robe, the Crow, stepped out from the shelter of a clump of woods and walked straight toward the Lakotas. He asked in sign language that the life of his son be spared. He was willing to sacrifice himself and all the men of his party if the Lakotas would take his child and adopt him into their tribe. He had hardly finished making his request when he dropped to the ground with White Thunder's arrow in his heart. So it was that the son of Stabber became Yellow Robe. When the battle was over, it was discovered that the little boy had also been killed.[3]

The version of the story told by Rosebud added the detail that during the battle, White Thunder counted coup on the Crow chief (that is, he touched him with his lance during a face-to-face confrontation but did not kill him at that time – an act of extreme bravery). The Crow chief, Yellow Robe, begged for the life of his son: "Kill me but spare my son." It was out of respect for the man's bravery that White Thunder took the name Yellow Robe. Rosebud noted that two endings to this story were remembered. In one, White Thunder spares the chief's son; in the other, he kills them both.

I recently learned another version of the story, told to me by Luke Yellow Robe,[4] in which the Lakotas and the Crows decided to end their constant killing of one another by giving exclusive hunting rights to the Yellowstone region to whoever was the victor in hand-to-hand combat to the death. White Thunder represented the Lakotas, and Yellow Robe represented the Crows. After White Thunder had been declared the victor, he said to the assembled Crows, "I will take the name of your brave headman, Yellow Robe. We will carry his name forever."[5] Years later, when Chauncey Yellow Robe was working at the Rapid City Indian School, he received a letter from the Crow chieftain's relatives asking to visit him. They related the story of the battle and said they would like to meet the members of the Lakota family that bore their ancestor's name.

Rosebud remembered receiving a phone call in the 1930s from Yellow Robes descended from the Crow chief. Visiting New York City, they had found Rosebud's name listed as Yellow Robe in the phone book. She invited them to her home, where they recounted their version of the event, which was similar to the story as Rosebud had heard it from her father.

Another family legend, told by Rosebud, related that Yellow Robe, the Lakota, was wounded in a battle and had an arrow point lodged in his hip that caused him much pain, especially during rainy weather. One day he shot an owl with an arrow but released it as quickly as he could. The wound was not fatal, for the owl soon flew away. That night, Yellow Robe dreamed that the owl released him from his arrow wound. He awoke next morning free of pain and found a portion of an arrow in his bed of buffalo robes. From that day forward, Yellow Robe prohibited anyone in his band from harming owls, believing that they offered him special protection.

Yellow Robe lived in a time of tremendous social upheaval. The rules of life that had guided his people from the earliest remembered days on the Great Plains were no longer reliable. One could win many battles and yet lose the only one that mattered – survival. An economy based mainly on the buffalo was quickly coming to an end, for the United States government not only condoned but encouraged the slaughter of millions of buffalo. The policy of exterminating the buffalo was adopted to facilitate the construction of railroads. U.S. military troops under Gen. William T. Sherman backed the railroad's policy, since the destruction of the buffalo would force the northern Plains Indians into dependency on the federal government and hasten their settlement on reservations, where they could be transformed into farmers. Thus the railroads and the Indians were locked in a battle that the Indians were doomed to lose. The Lakotas realized that the railroads would drive away the buffalo and other game as well as bring more and more settlers to the Plains. Their way of life was under siege.

By 1867, when Chauncey, Rosebud's father, was born, the rail line had just been completed from coast to coast; the buffalo had been decimated; and food, clothing, and shelter were in short supply. The next year many of the Lakota leaders, Yellow Robe among them, signed the Treaty of 1868 at Fort Laramie. Since none of the Lakota chiefs could read or understand a word of English, they had no choice but to trust the treaty commissioners. In return for signing the treaty, the commissioners promised that the United States government would provide the Lakotas with food, clothing, and shelter, as well as education for their children.

The Treaty of 1868 for the first time put boundaries around what became known as the Great Sioux Reservation. This reduction of Lakota territorial claims ultimately led to the loss of much of their land, including the Black Hills, where gold was discovered in 1874. White fortune-seekers swarmed to the Black Hills in violation of the treaty, and the U.S. Army was unable to keep them out. Tensions mounted in 1875 as the government attempted to negotiate a purchase of the Black Hills, and when those negotiations failed, an order was sent to all the Lakotas to return within the reservation boundaries by January 31, 1876, or be considered hostile to the government. A huge military campaign was mounted, and on June 17, Gen. George Crook's forces clashed with the Lakotas on the Rosebud River in Montana. Neither side was victorious, and Crook retreated south to Wyoming to await reinforcements.

During this difficult time, Yellow Robe seems to have been dedicated to peace. He was mentioned, for example, in a telegram sent by Sherman to Gen. Alfred Terry on June 6, 1876: "Couriers from the Red Cloud Agency reported at Laramie yesterday that Yellow Robe arrived at the agency six days from the hostile camp. He said that 1800 lodges were on the Rosebud and about to leave for Powder River below the point of Crazy Horse fight and have about 3,000 warriors."[6]

The summer's military campaign culminated in the Battle of the Little Bighorn on June 25, 1876. Family tradition reports that Yellow Robe was prominent in the battle. But the victory over Lt. Col. George A. Custer and his Seventh Cavalry was a hollow one. With the destruction of the buffalo and continued harassment by military troops, the Lakotas had no choice but to return to the agencies on their reservation.[7]

The years of painful adaptation to reservation life resulted in the development of new economic strategies, including cattle raising and wage labor at the agencies. But progress was intermittent. Some of the government agents siphoned off rations to sell for their own profit while keeping their wards on near-starvation diets. Moreover, up to this time the Lakotas had lived in portable tipis, moving their villages frequently. Without an understanding of how to live in and maintain permanent housing, the people fell victim to poor hygiene, enabling disease – notably tuberculosis – to spread among them.[8]

Education in white ways seemed the only answer to reservation problems. The Indian boarding school at Carlisle, Pennsylvania, established in 1879 by General Richard H. Pratt, offered one solution: total immersion of Indian children in the ways of the majority culture. Pratt designed the school to provide Indian students with a basic education and to instruct them in domestic and trade skills.[9]

Before the Lakota headmen would send their children to Carlisle, however, Pratt had to convince them that it would be to their advantage. In 1883, at Rosebud Agency, Dakota Territory, some forty chiefs and prominent men were called to a meeting. Pratt explained to them the purposes of the school and urged them to send their children. Spotted Tail answered for all: "The White people are all thieves and liars and we refuse to send our children because we do not want them to learn such things. . . . The government knew that gold was there [in the Black Hills] and it took the land from us without giving us its value. . . . The government has always cheated us and we do not want our children to learn to do that way."

Pratt replied by turning the Lakota chief's argument around: "You are the head of these people because you have a strong mind, but Spotted Tail, you cannot read or write. You sign papers and do not know what you sign. . . . If you had been educated like the Whites, you might have known there was gold in the Black Hills . . . and might be there . . . now directing [your people] to get the gold out of the ground." After extolling the practical value of literacy and the benefits of education, Pratt came around to the theme of changing times:

You have seen how the White people are coming more and more. . . . There is no more chance for your people to keep themselves away from the Whites. You are compelled to meet them. Your children will have to live with them. . . . Your own welfare while you live and the welfare of your children after you, and all your interests in every way, *demand* that your children should have the same education that the White man has, that they should speak his language and know just how the White man lives. . . . I propose not only to take your children to the school at Carlisle, but I shall send them out to work and to live among the White people, and into the White man's home and schools so that as boys and girls they will be coming into the same classes with White boys and girls and will so learn to know each other, and this will take away their prejudice against the Whites and take away the prejudice of the Whites against your people, and it is the only way to remove such prejudice.

According to Pratt's account, after his speech the chiefs agreed to his request without further argument. "It is all right," Spotted Tail said. "We are going to give you all the children you want." [10]

This was not Pratt's first visit to Rosebud. Standing Bear and some of the other chiefs had sent their sons and grandsons to Carlisle three years before. Some of those boys had died there, and their fathers were angry and suspicious, but Standing Bear had visited the school and had come back telling wonderful tales of what the boys were doing. His son, now called Luther Standing Bear, returned to the reservation with Pratt and demonstrated what he had learned. He had spoken well of the school, reported that the students received good food and warm clothes, and did his best to persuade his people to allow other boys and girls to return to Carlisle with him.[11]

Yellow Robe agreed to send his two sons to the school. The older boy, age fifteen, was named Kills in the Woods (*Cha̧' ówichakte*), in commemoration of Yellow Robe's victory over the Crow chief. At Carlisle, he would receive the name Chauncey. The younger son, named Search the Enemy, at Carlisle was named Richard. As a chief, Yellow Robe knew it was his duty to lead the way by sending his boys to a white school. Others would follow his example. To give his own children was the only thing he could do for the salvation of his people.

By sending his own sons to be educated, Yellow Robe began the process of combining Lakota and white ways. He hoped that they would learn the skills necessary for living in the rapidly changing world and, upon returning, would teach others. Yellow Robe lived to the age of eighty-seven, and by the time of his death in 1914 he had seen the new era well under way.[12]

2

Chauncey Yellow Robe

Chauncey Yellow Robe remembered his childhood fondly, with a good dose of nostalgia.[1] He was born in the southern part of Montana, where his people were hunting buffalo. Among his early memories he recalled that his mother, Tachcawin (Deer Woman), had carried him on her back and that as her firstborn he was her favored child.[2] While he was still an infant, his family "gave a big feast"[3] and named him Kills in the Woods in memory of his father's victory over the Crow chief from whom he took the name Yellow Robe.

Chauncey remembered his grandfather and his grandmother, both of whom he characterized as "giant in stature and strength." He wrote of them:

They were my tutors in legends. Many hours I used to spend in their buffalo-hide tepees beside the bright campfire, listening to their strange stories that had been handed down for generations. I was expected to commit to memory all these stories that I might be able to relate them to my children. I was taught to respect and reverence the Great Spirit, which was an essential to this life, to know the importance of the past history of the tribe and to study the great and inspiring deeds of the famous chiefs, warriors and medicine men.

Chauncey recalled as well his training in the necessities of life for a Lakota male: making bows and arrows, riding ponies bareback, foot racing, wrestling, and swimming. It was important, he wrote, to learn to endure all kinds of hardships: "Sometimes during a morning of winter blizzard my father used to wake me up out of my warm bed of buffalo robes and dare me to go out and lay down in the deep snow and roll in it 'as I had

come in the world.' This was not as a punishment, but a test in endurance."
He learned the art of hunting by accompanying his father. "Many times,"
Chauncey remembered, "I have helped him to lift a deer on his back or drag
one home on the snow. Living next to nature and by close observation, I
became familiar with the peculiar characteristics and habits of the animals
and the birds."

For a Lakota boy, killing his first buffalo was a major step toward man-
hood. Chauncey killed his first buffalo one autumn near the Black Hills
when he was staying with his uncle Iron Plume and his aunt Catch the
Bear. The camp was on the Belle Fourche River, where Chauncey's duty
was to look after the family's large pony herd. Chauncey recounted the
event:

One day while my uncle was away, it was announced throughout the camp that a
large herd of buffaloes was moving towards it, and all the able-bodied men as well
as boys were preparing for the chase. I could not resist from going. I kept my eyes
on Aunt and when she went out of the tepee to hang up some buffalo meat to dry,
I picked up my arrow quiver and a piece of buffalo rawhide rope and, running to
the ponies on the field, caught my fleet-footed pony and joined the hunting party.

When we were out five or six miles from the camp we saw the buffalo herd,
something like two or three thousand, calves and all, grazing on a broad stretch of
low land. We made an advance towards the buffaloes behind the hills and then we
made a charge upon them, shouting our war whoops as we went. The great buffalo
herd stampeded toward the west, a thick cloud of dust rising behind them. My
pony was so excited that I could not control him. Reaching the buffaloes through
the smoke of dust, I was right among them. They rubbed against my side as they
ran. My pony turned his ears down and raced with the herd. I was afraid at first,
thinking if I fell off my pony I would be trampled to death by the buffaloes.

Finally I gained confidence in myself and drew my bow and arrows out from the
quiver at my belt and sent the first arrow into a yearling buffalo on my right. She
staggered and dropped out of the stampede, and so I shot another arrow into her.
My last arrow was effective. She finally lay down and died, killed with the bow and
arrows I, myself, had made. With much pleasurable emotions within my heart to
see the dead buffalo before me, I dismounted and tied my pony to sagebrush and
skinned the buffalo the way my father and uncle had taught me to do. My intention
was to pack the whole buffalo on my pony, but I realized it was impossible to do
so for I rode bareback. I only took the hide and hindquarter.

First I threw the buffalo hide across the pony's back. He smelled the blood, and
how he bucked and kicked until he threw it off. I took some blood and rubbed it

on his nose and face; this made him submissive, and I had no more trouble with him. I loaded the meat on his back and rode him for home. I reached the camp late in the evening, unpacked the load from my pony by the tepee and turned the pony loose.

I was thirsty, hungry, and tired from the long ride. I entered the tepee. My uncle and aunt greeted me gladly, for they had begun to worry about me. Uncle returned before I did; he had killed one or two big buffaloes on that day. My aunt was just roasting one whole side of buffalo ribs over the fire. I lay down on a bed of buffalo robes resting myself while they were slicing the delicious roasted ribs for supper. In the meantime, my uncle asked me about the chase. I told him it was a big success; everybody killed one or two buffaloes. He said, "Did you kill one?" I told him I did. I went out and brought in my trophy of the chase. They were greatly surprised and pleased with the success of my first buffalo chase.

Chauncey told Rosebud that when old Yellow Robe heard that his son, Kills in the Woods, had killed his first buffalo all alone, he ordered the camp crier to proclaim the news throughout the village; then, as a thanksgiving sacrifice, he gave away one of his horses. Since in those days a man's wealth was counted by the number of ponies in his possession, it was customary to give away horses. The gift was all the more important because it was always made to a needy person who was unable to reciprocate.

One morning not long after the buffalo hunt, Kills in the Woods awoke to find his world covered with several inches of fine snow. The tipis, smoke-stained the day before, were now wrapped in white mantles. He had been looking forward to the first heavy snowfall with more eagerness than usual, for this year he had constructed a sled from ash wood, fashioning runners from the ribs of a buffalo and using the hide to cover the frame.[4]

In Kills in the Woods's opinion, there was no lighter or swifter sled in the whole camp, although four other boys had also built sleds of their own and were as proud as he of their handiwork. For weeks they had all been wishing for snow so that they might prove the superiority of their sleds. So this morning when Kills in the Woods beheld the glistening landscape, he tumbled from his bed of buffalo robes, hurriedly ate some of the meat his mother had roasted for breakfast, and, taking his precious sled, rushed from the tipi. On a hill at the lower end of the village a number of boys were already coasting.

The boys' competition had aroused considerable interest in the camp. It had been decided that the owners of the five sleds should race them in order to determine which was the speediest. As each contestant approached the hill, he was greeted with a chorus of challenges and pelted with snowballs. Although a keen sense of rivalry existed among the boys, it was the spirit of fun that prevailed.

All the other contestants had arrived by the time Kills in the Woods had made a couple of trial runs down the hill. Then the five boys lined up behind their sleds, ready for the race. Down the hill and clearly visible against the white background, a brilliantly painted red stake had been driven into the snow. The first boy who passed it was to jerk the stake from its place.

At a given signal the sleds shot forward, faster and faster over the sparkling surface; swift as birds they flew. Kills in the Woods and Running Wolf were leading, shoulder to shoulder. As the red stake loomed up ahead, Kills in the Woods swerved sharply to the right to avoid striking it; at the same moment Running Wolf swerved to the left. Both boys gripped the stake tightly and held on. Thus locked together, the two sleds sped on down the hill, each boy so intent upon trying to pull the stake from the other's grasp that they did not look where they were going, and before they knew what was happening, they had plunged head first into a snowdrift. By the time they had pulled themselves out and wiped their faces, they were surrounded by a crowd of laughing boys all shouting at once.

After much discussion, it was agreed the winner should be chosen by a snowball fight in which all the boys would join, the two sides to be headed by Kills in the Woods and Running Wolf. The stake was placed on top of a huge snowball in the center of an open space. The side securing the stake would win.

In relating this little episode later in life, Chauncey ended by saying, with a humorous twinkle in his dark eyes, "Running Wolf and his band won that fight, but I still believed my sled was the best."[5]

Chauncey described the first time he saw a white man as a significant event in his life:

At one of the trading posts on the Missouri river where my parents went to trade, my brother and I were out playing around the camp and saw a strange looking man coming towards us. The man had long hair and a beard and wore a large hat and fringed buckskin suit. He carried a musket on his shoulder. I could not distinguish as to whether he was a man or an animal of some kind. As he came nearer to us, I concluded he was an evil spirit. I gave a loud scream, leaving my brother behind me and ran back to my father in the tepee, threw my arms around his neck, cried and told him what I had seen, but he laughed and said that it was a White man, and told us not to go very far away or the White man would kidnap us. Since then, I have learned not to fear the White man.

Thus I spent my boyhood days with my people on the great plains until I was fifteen years of age. My dreams for glory in the Indian world vanished from my vision. Against my own wishes, I was given to General R. H. Pratt to take to school in the far east.[6]

Chauncey's younger brother, Search the Enemy (Richard Yellow Robe), reported that it had been their father's decision to send the brothers to Carlisle. At first, Richard later wrote, he did not want to go, but he obeyed his father's wish that the boys go to school and learn white people's ways.[7]

Kills in the Woods and Search the Enemy, with forty-eight other boys and girls, left Rosebud Agency in November 1883. They would form the fourth class to enter Carlisle. At first, the journey in the "little iron houses on tracks" was an exciting adventure, but at the end of the third day Chauncey was tired and stiff, for he was not used to such close confinement. The older boys had told the younger ones quite solemnly that they must sit very straight, for if they moved to the left or to the right, the train would tip in that direction.[8]

Eating was problematical. The children had no experience with cutlery, and so in the dining cars or at railroad station lunchrooms, they put their food into their blankets to eat later. It was only after three days and nights of rushing past villages and through cities filled with white people that they arrived at their destination.

"On the way to the east," Chauncey wrote, "I wore my full Indian costume, long hair, feathers, blanket, leggings, moccasins, and painted face, not knowing a word of English, not having seen a book or a schoolhouse before."[9]

They arrived on November 20, and before being stripped of their Indian dress, the students were taken to be photographed. Chauncey later said that this was for curiosity's sake. The experience was terrifying because when the photographer pointed a queer-looking black machine at him, he thought he was going to be shot. Since he had never before seen or even heard of a camera, he was badly frightened, but he obeyed the interpreter, sitting stiffly erect and expecting the shot at any moment. After a few tense moments, during which the photographer was behind a black cloth, the silence was broken by a click. He was startled at the sound but felt nothing. When he was told that the picture had been taken, he could not understand how anyone could take his picture without touching him. Incredulity gave place to amazement when on the following day his photograph arrived. It seemed like magic: the mysterious box had produced an exact likeness, far different from the pictographic drawings of the Lakotas.[10]

The children were next bathed and dressed in "civilized" clothes that were new to them, and uncomfortable. The boys had their hair cut short, which was particularly traumatic, for among the Lakotas cutting the hair was a sign of mourning. When Kills in the Woods's hair was cut, his first thought was that his mother must have died. He was the first of the students to have his hair cut, and he assumed that the barber cut the other boys' hair out of respect for his mother.[11]

With clothing and hairstyle like those of white students, it was now necessary for the children to receive English names. On the third day at Carlisle, Kills in the Woods entered the classroom to find the blackboard covered with columns of names. The interpreter pronounced the names and explained to the class that each student should choose one from those on the board, and from then on he would be known by that name. Kills in the Woods was given a stick and told to point to the name of his choice. He selected Chauncey, quite possibly because it started with the same sound as his Lakota name, *Chą'ówichakte*, or because, as he told Rosebud years later, he thought it sounded French, and the first white people he had known were French traders. The teacher then wrote the name on a piece of white tape, sewed it in the back of his coat collar, and erased the name from the blackboard so that no other boy could take it. He was then legally registered as Chauncey Yellow Robe, the government having ruled that Indian children must take their father's name as a surname. In this way Kills in the Woods became Chauncey Yellow Robe. His classmates sometimes called him Timber or Wounded, from Kills in the Woods.

As with a name, Chauncey was asked to choose among Christian faiths. Without really understanding denominational differences, he followed the majority of students and was baptized in the Episcopal Church.

The first six months Chauncey spent at Carlisle were the saddest of his life as he tried to accustom himself to this strange new environment. The pungent odor of wood smoke escaping from the stove in the center of the classroom awakened memories of his old home and his free life on the prairies. His clipped head felt queer; he kept running his hand over it and wishing for the long braids of which he had been so proud. The close-fitting wool garments scratched his skin, and the heavy shoes made his feet feel like boards. He longed to be able to speak the Lakota language freely again. Every fiber of his being cried out in protest against the harsh, clipped English he was obliged to speak. He wrote of that time, "Never had I experienced such homesickness as I did then. How many times have I watched the western sky and cried within my broken heart, wishing to see my father and mother again and be free on the plains."[12]

When the children arrived from the reservations, most of them knew no English, but they were forbidden to speak their native language. At first they were given slates and paper and coloring materials to communicate through word pictures, the same pictographic methods they had observed their elders using in hide painting. As the students learned to write in English, sometimes they added explanatory words to their picture stories. Unfortunately, only a very few pictographic drawings made at Carlisle from the period 1879 through 1885 have been preserved, although many were created.[13] The boys and girls were also exposed to white people's art forms. As a result, they rapidly developed three-dimensional representation in their drawing and abandoned the pictographic style.

At first Chauncey was shy. He distrusted his teachers, in spite of their kindness, until he learned enough of their language and ways to appreciate them. His reserve gradually gave way to confidence. He often recalled his mother's admonition: "Go, and like a warrior, be brave, remembering always your people and their great need of you." Little by little, as his self-confidence increased, he entered fully into the routine of student life, in and out of the classroom. The gnawing ache of homesickness became less painful, and he kept always in mind the purpose for which he was studying.

Chauncey never forgot his first Christmas at Carlisle. He enjoyed the big turkey dinner, and the Christmas tree, with its shimmering tinsel and twinkling lights, filled him with wonder. When he was given some of the presents that were piled under the tree, he was delighted, but the color and sparkle of the tree itself fascinated him most. That first Christmas, little more than a month after his arrival at Carlisle, he failed altogether to understand the religious significance of the day, and until he learned that the celebration occurred only once a year, he wondered when the next Christmas Day would come around.[14]

As Chauncey's knowledge of English improved and his understanding of the new customs increased, his earnestness, sincerity, and gentleness, combined with a keen sense of humor, attracted Pratt's attention. Not until summer vacation, however, when he took Chauncey and a number of other students on a camping trip, did Pratt really come to know the young man. Once away from the school and out in a natural environment, every vestige of reticence disappeared, and Chauncey's self-reliance became evident. Each boy had his regular tasks to perform about the camp, but in order to test Chauncey, Pratt began to rely more and more upon him, giving him added responsibilities. Chauncey willingly accepted these extra duties, trying hard to carry them out in a manner satisfactory to his teacher. Both Pratt and Chauncey were ardent fishermen, and they spent many days of that summer together with rod and line. Soon a friendship began that inspired the young man and become a source of satisfaction for Pratt.[15]

An integral part of the educational system that Pratt designed for Carlisle was the "outing" system, in which students spent their summers working on farms or in businesses. From Pratt's perspective, outing had the dual advantage of providing work experience in white society and preventing students from returning to the reservation environment.

Chauncey's first experience with outing took place during his second summer at the school. A Quaker farmer who lived some distance from Carlisle had written to request a boy to help him on his farm, and Pratt chose Chauncey for the job. The trip required several hours of train travel, so he started off one morning soon after breakfast. He was given a lunch and told to eat it on the train when he was hungry. Being young and healthy, he soon felt the need of it, but timidity kept him from opening the package in front of strangers. With each passing hour his hunger increased; he fingered the brown paper package in his lap, and his mouth watered when he thought of the food it contained, but nothing could induce him to open it.

Late that afternoon Chauncey arrived at his destination. The farmer and his wife received him kindly. At suppertime he took his place at the table but was unable to eat. It was the first time he had ever been in a white man's home, and the strangeness of the surroundings robbed him of all self-reliance. He was bashful and frightened. Although he was famished, the sight and smell of food made him dizzy, and he could not force himself to taste a mouthful. That night when all was quiet, Chauncey sat up in bed and ate the lunch he had carried all the way from Carlisle. Never before had anything tasted so good. In the days that followed he was obliged to overcome his timidity, for he soon discovered that the work of a farmhand cannot be done on an empty stomach.

Later, Chauncey's summers were spent in a variety of ways: working on farms; attending the Moody Summer School at Northfield, Massachusetts; and serving as an athletic instructor at resorts along the Atlantic seacoast.

In 1893, Chauncey was chosen – doubtless on Pratt's recommendation –

as a representative of North American Indians at the Congress of Nations held to celebrate the opening of the World's Columbian Exposition in Chicago. One evening as he was watching the people in the Indian Hall – a museum display of artifacts and life-size dioramas depicting the native cultures of North America – he was approached by a woman who asked him why he had not painted his face. Though dressed in full Plains Indian costume, Chauncey had left his face unpainted, as he usually did. Apparently, to this woman an Indian was not an Indian unless his face was painted, and she said as much. Chauncey looked at her, maintaining a very serious expression but with keen eyes that began to sparkle with merriment. The woman was beautifully dressed; her pretty face was cleverly rouged and her eyebrows thinly penciled. Chauncey, whose sense of humor was always in evidence, noted these details; then, assuming an expression of surprised embarrassment, he said, "Perhaps the lady would be so kind as to lend me her make-up kit." The lady was most obliging. Taking her proffered mirror, Chauncey deftly applied eyebrow pencil and lipstick to parts of his face where they never before had been used. When he had obtained the desired effect, he handed back the articles, saying in a quiet voice, "You are right, paint makes the Indian – now I am a real one."[16]

Native peoples were variously represented at the fair. In addition to the museum displays, groups from throughout North America were brought to Chicago, where they constructed traditional dwellings, danced, and put on other performances for tourists. Buffalo Bill (William F.) Cody brought his Wild West Show to Chicago, locating it near the entrance to the exposition, and his performers – mostly Lakotas – pitched their tipis on the fair's Midway Plaisance. All these representations of the Native past were in stark contrast to the U.S. government's Indian school exhibit: a model Indian school was constructed, and students from the various boarding schools, including Carlisle, demonstrated to visitors through recitations and performances the progress of American Indians in education.

Between Buffalo Bill and the Indian school exhibit, fairgoers received vastly different messages about American Indians, with the Wild West Show being far more popular – though not with Chauncey. He had already had some familiarity with Buffalo Bill; in 1890 he had gone to Washington DC to serve as an interpreter at an inquiry made by the Office of Indian Affairs into the treatment of Indians traveling with Buffalo Bill's show.[17] Chauncey's recognition then of the extent to which his people were being exploited and sensationalized kindled in him a lifelong antipathy for such performances.

Chauncey graduated with honor from Carlisle in the class of 1895. To conform to Pratt's expectations, he had submerged his Indianness, for Carlisle's message was loud and clear: success in education and in life required that the Indian become white in thought and deed. For twelve years he had worked and studied, assuming the customs and habits of the majority culture along with its methods of thought – but throughout, he preserved Lakota values and language.[18]

Chauncey's father had sent him to Carlisle as Kills in the Woods, a Lakota warrior, to learn whatever he could to help his people. He needed to learn to decipher treaties, to find ways for economic betterment, and to choose the best that white education could offer him for the good of his people. After completing his studies, Chauncey returned home.[19]

He first intended to enter the ministry, believing that in that capacity he could render the greatest service. After a few months spent with his father visiting many Indian communities in South Dakota, however, he clearly saw his duty to his people and realized that, especially for the younger generation, the urgent need was for teachers of their own blood. Reservation conditions had not improved significantly during the years he had been gone. The failed promise of the Ghost Dance and the massacre of Big Foot's band at Wounded Knee in 1890 had left the Lakotas disillusioned. Disease, resulting from their ignorance of sanitation in permanent housing, combined with illiteracy and a lack of vocational outlets, threatened to destroy the Lakotas as a people.

Speaking of this period in his life, Chauncey said, "My heart ached when I saw how my people were suffering. I could not go back East to the seminary. They needed me." Putting aside his ambition to become a minister, he applied to the Bureau of Indian Affairs and soon entered the government school system in order to "teach his people to see both the good of the old life and the good of the new."[20] For a while he went back to Carlisle as assistant disciplinarian (boy's dean). In 1897, after a year spent at schools in Santee, Nebraska, and Fort Lewis, Colorado, he was appointed boys' disciplinarian at Fort Shaw Indian School in Montana. When he arrived at Fort Shaw, he bought a bicycle with solid paper tires, but he soon learned that the western roads were, as he put it, "uncivilized" for bicycles.

As disciplinarian, one of Chauncey's many duties was to receive the boys as they came in from their reservations. At first, forgetful of the conditions under which they lived, he was disgusted by their dirty, vermin-infested bodies, but he soon reminded himself that he too had once been in the same condition. Firmness was of the greatest importance in executing his duties, but he tempered it with sympathetic understanding that never failed to win him the respect, at least, and the friendship, at best, of the boys in his charge.

Quite often, unable to endure the life at school, boys would run away, and it was up to Chauncey to find them and bring them back. His attitude at such times was very much like the father who felt obliged to spank his little boy for being naughty: "My son, this hurts me more than it does you." Because he vividly remembered his first few weeks at Carlisle and how he had longed for his old home, he did not blame those heartsick children, but he knew that they had to be returned to school for their own good. A runaway boy was usually wise enough not to go directly to his home; instead, he would flee to friends or relatives living far away. Finding him sometimes necessitated two or three days' travel for Chauncey, inquiring first at one place and then at another until he finally located the truant. Then, more often than not, his troubles had only begun, for Indian parents could not bear to think that their children were so unhappy. Few of them understood the necessity of learning white ways. They had sent their children to school in the first place because in a weak moment they had been persuaded by a missionary or by their chief. But if going to school made their children unhappy, they should not have to go. It took all of Chauncey's persuasiveness to convince parents that siding with their truant son was a mistake. In the end, Chauncey's sympathy and gentleness usually won out, and he would ride off with the child beside him. When he failed to receive the parents' permission to take a child back, however, further action to return the youngster to school was necessary.

At Fort Shaw, Chauncey filled the positions of both industrial teacher and disciplinarian. He was transferred next to Sisseton, South Dakota, then to Genoa, Nebraska, "having been promoted each transfer."[21] He returned to Carlisle as assistant disciplinarian in 1898, where one of his duties was to visit patrons of the school. He was an effective communicator and exemplified the success of Indian education. His "Sioux tongue," wrote one Carlisle official, "will not bend easily to some of our English twists and turns, but this is no drawback to him."[22]

Chauncey again left Carlisle in August 1898 to return to Colorado as disciplinarian at the Fort Lewis School.[23] The next year, however, citing an adverse reaction to the altitude, he went to South Dakota to recuperate.[24]

In 1900 he returned to Fort Shaw, Montana. A presentation on the need for off-reservation boarding schools that he made that year at the Grand Opera House in Great Falls, Montana, attracted attention: "His remarks were earnest and forcibly delivered . . . and the whole audience frequently applauded his expressions. He made a plea for non-reservation schools for the Indians. He eloquently urged that the Indians are anxious for communication with the Whites and for citizenship." Citing himself as the product of a nonreservation school, Chauncey declared: "Five years ago I left Carlisle . . . and I am still on the warpath toward civilization."[25]

In 1905, at the start of fall semester, the Rapid City Indian School offered Chauncey an appointment as an industrial arts instructor, allowing him to return to South Dakota.[26] He remained there, first as a teacher and then as boys' disciplinarian, for the next twenty-three years. He also coached the boys' basketball team.[27] Students at the school remembered him as strict but fair. Those who followed his directives spoke of his kindly advice and wise counsel; those who did not decried the military punishment that he dealt out to unruly boys.

Many of his own people misunderstood Chauncey's attitude. In their opinion he was working for the whites and deliberately undermining Lakota values. They failed to appreciate his point of view. Chauncey believed he was helping the students learn the fundamentals of living with the dominant culture. By encouragement and example he sought to cultivate among the younger generation the ambition to succeed in the white people's world. Yet he also believed in preserving Lakota values and traditions. On camping trips with some of the students, Chauncey would reveal a more approachable side of his personality by telling stories about his youth. A dramatic storyteller, he loved to relate the tale of a bear hunt in which he had participated when he returned home to the Black Hills after his years at Carlisle. His voice was low-pitched and clear as he began:

It was early in the fall of the year. Fifteen or twenty young men were given permission to go out on a hunting trip. One morning before sunrise, equipped with camp supplies, rifles, and long hunting knives, they left the reservation. They traveled all that day without seeing a single bear track. It was nearing sunset when they reached an excellent campsite on a bluff overlooking a river. Before long the ponies were hobbled, fires lighted, and the camp was astir with preparations for the evening meal. Suddenly, there was a shout from a young man who had been detailed to fetch water from the river. He had seen bear tracks in the mud along the bank. Hurriedly the young men finished their supper, extinguished the fires, and rolled themselves in their blankets to await the bear. Every hour a new man was chosen to act as lookout. About midnight, it was Chauncey's turn. Taking his rifle and hunting knife, he slid down the bluff. "Naturally," he would say with a broad smile, "I hoped I would be the lucky one. I sat down with my back against a tree with my rifle close at hand. I peered into the darkness but could see nothing. I was thinking about my sweetheart away back in the East when I heard a slight noise behind me. I thought it was one of the boys to relieve me and paid no attention. But the noise continued. Suddenly out of the darkness loomed a big black object. I jumped to my feet, only to be knocked down with a terrific blow. I struggled upright wondering what I should do. My rifle was beyond my reach. Again I was knocked to the ground. I felt the bear's claws rip the flesh on my shoulder. Stunned, frightened, I struggled to rise. I knew it was the end of Chauncey Yellow Robe. Suddenly I thought of the hunting knife in my belt. With a last supreme effort, I jerked the knife from its sheath and rose unsteadily to one knee. The bear reared on his hind legs for the final stroke. As he did so, I plunged my knife into his heart. Then – in my struggle so extreme – I awoke."[28]

Chauncey often told this story, invariably deriving much pleasure from the expressions of surprise on his listeners' faces. He was gentle, honest, and sincere. Physically, he was about five feet, ten inches tall and carried himself perfectly erect, as poised as an athlete. His relatives and friends remembered the dignity and strength of his bearing, together with the magnetic personality that made him beloved by many. He spoke in straight-forward though Lakota-accented English, pausing frequently, emphasizing his words with gestures and facial expressions that fascinated his listeners. Chauncey's ability to hold the attention of his audience was due in part to the graphic manner of his speech and to his own huge enjoyment of what he was saying.

3

Life in South Dakota

In 1905, Chauncey Yellow Robe fell in love with Lillian Belle Springer, a nurse at the Rapid City Indian School. Born in Crookston, Minnesota, August 7, 1885, to Henry and Emma Sprenger, Lillie and her family moved in 1888 to Tacoma, Washington, where she was reared and went to school. Members of her family had emigrated to the United States from the German-speaking city of Neftenbach, Switzerland, in 1854.[1]

Having decided on nursing as a career, Lillie studied at the Maria Bilard Deaconess Hospital Nurses' Training School in Spokane, Washington. She graduated in 1902 and for a time was employed by a local doctor. But she had inherited a pioneer spirit from her father, who had left his home in Minnesota and prospected for gold on the Klondike. Seeking an adventure of her own, Lillie sat for the civil service exam in nursing, knowing that if she passed, she could be assigned to a post in Panama or with Indians in the United States, depending on the needs of the moment.

Although her parents were opposed to her leaving home, Lillie was twenty-one years old and could not be forced to stay in Tacoma. Eventually she overcame her parents' opposition, and in July 1905 she was offered an appointment at the Rapid City Indian School in South Dakota. She wrote to her friend Clara Henneman: "Papa thought it a fine chance. . . . I telephoned my acceptance. . . . I just took the exams for fun to see if I could pass. I decided that I could work myself up higher there than just by staying here and doing private work." She signed a one-year contract and left Tacoma for Rapid City in August 1905. Lillie regarded the assignment as a marvelous lark; she confided to friends that this was to be her "great adventure" and that she would return at the end of the school year.[2]

The Rapid City Indian School lacked most of the essentials to operate an infirmary, but Lillie was undaunted and worked diligently those first few months to make the best of the situation. According to the family story Rosebud told, Lillie first met Chauncey as he rushed into the infirmary carrying a young Indian student whose badly injured left arm was bleeding profusely and dangling at his side. All the beds were occupied at the time and Lillie led Chauncey to her own room, located just off the infirmary, where she prepared her bed for the injured boy.

Not long thereafter, Chauncey and Lillie fell in love and would let nothing keep them apart. Theirs was an immediate and intense attraction, but it violated the rule that prohibited fraternization between Indian and white faculty.[3] For that reason, their courtship in the beginning consisted mainly of writing notes and pinning them in each other's coats in the faculty cloakroom. They continued to write notes to each other throughout their twenty-one years of marriage. Love notes were hidden in various places in their home, and Rosebud remembered her mother's pleasure at finding them.

Years later Chauncey told his daughters that in Lillie he had found a woman who was gentle, empathetic, and practical, one with whom he felt compelled to share his life. They were a striking couple: he, dark and handsome with classic Lakota features; she, a Germanic blonde and quite beautiful. Despite the concerns of family and friends, they married within the year. Chauncey had convinced the administration that this was a special union of two people who could make an interracial marriage work.

The wedding took place on Tuesday, May 22, 1906, at the Harney Hotel; a Reverend Mr. Sparling officiated, and Jesse F. House, superintendent of the Rapid City Indian School, gave Lillie away.[4] No member of either family was present, but a small group of friends congratulated the couple and joyously wished them well. Chauncey's customary presence of mind deserted him on his wedding day, however, and Lillie derived much pleasure thereafter from teasing him about it. He had been so excited that he neglected to order the food for the wedding breakfast and reception, so they were obliged to take whatever the hotel could provide. The fruit was prunes – which Lillie could not endure. It was then, she always laughingly declared, that she realized her mistake in marrying Chauncey Yellow Robe.

The couple were driven to and from the wedding by their friends Ned and May Peck in one of the first horseless carriages in Rapid City. From the hotel they were taken to the railroad station.[5] They spent their honeymoon in South Dakota at Hot Springs, Deadwood, and Sylvan Lake.

Inevitably, the marriage of an Indian man and white woman was not without criticism. Even Lillie's friend Clara wrote to her in surprise at the news. Her reply, postmarked Rapid City, September 14, 1906, was written on Chauncey's stationery, embossed with a bow and arrow:

So you are surprised because I married into a different race and you think it awful. But it is not – in years to come people will not think it so.

Mr. Robe is more than my equal in every way. I am proud to own his name – he is of a good family & I am, so why shouldn't our offspring be bright, intelligent and healthy. I do not see why you feel sorry – I do not. The folks are perfectly satisfied and look at it the way I do. Since we have been married, we have made a great many friends – people here admire Mr. Robe greatly – he is respected anywhere as much as anyone.

Remember I did not have to marry an Indian. At this same time there were two White men here in Rapid that cared enough about me to make me their wife – but I did not love them – and how could I be happy with either. It seems as if God's hand has been leading us – because we both tried so hard not to care for each other. And we are so very happy now – I just can't be thankful enough.

Chauncey and Lillian seem not to have met prejudice, either in Rapid City or on their travels, with the exception of a single incident that occurred in 1913. While attending a meeting in Denver they overheard a threatening comment in the hotel bar about an Indian man with a white woman. That night they piled furniture against the door of their room.[6]

On February 26, 1907, Lillie gave birth to the couple's first child, a girl. That very day, sitting at his desk at the Rapid City Indian School, Chauncey wrote glowingly to Pratt, his teacher and mentor. He confided that he had been so certain his first child would be a boy that he and his wife had not even chosen a girl's name. Chauncey told Pratt that it was only as he was writing a letter to his father, on the Rosebud Reservation, that he decided Rosebud would be a fine name for his firstborn. Later, Lillie wrote to Clara that Rosebud had been enrolled at the agency and allotted 160 acres of reservation land.[7] When Rosebud was six months old, the Yellow Robes made one of their many visits to Tacoma to visit Lillie's parents. Of those trips, Chauncey later wrote to Pratt, "It is always a pleasure to go and visit my wife's family for they always treat me like a Prince."[8]

While living in the government house on the grounds of the Indian school, the Yellow Robes completed their family with the addition of two more daughters. Chauncina was born on December 28, 1909, and named after her father, who had given up hope of having a son. Evelyn was born ten years later, on Christmas Day, after Lillie had become badly crippled with rheumatoid arthritis.

Employees at the Indian school enjoyed the convenience of a student-run laundry service. Students picked up and delivered laundry at the government houses. Bessie Cornelius was one of those students who frequently visited the Yellow Robe home.[9] She too was from a biracial family, but her father was white and her mother Indian, a kind of marriage more common on the reservations. Later on, she remembered the warmth of the Yellow Robe home, which she said always smelled of fresh baking. Although she used a wheelchair, Lillie moved about easily. Bessie recalled the loving relationship between Chauncey and Lillie, and Chauncey's keen sense of humor. He was always well dressed, wearing the celluloid collars that were then fashionable.[10] Lillie dressed fashionably, too, ordering her clothes from Chicago. Rosebud remembered that when friends came to dinner, the table setting usually included candlesticks.

Chauncey had hoped for a son to follow in his footsteps, but, accepting the fact that he had only daughters, he taught them as many Lakota traditions as he could. Rosebud recalled occasions when elderly Indians would visit the grounds of the Indian school and tell stories in the Lakota language. Chauncey would have Rosebud listen, even though she could not understand a word, and later he would retell the stories in English. The story about the fight at the Little Bighorn would forever stand out in her memory. The men would say that after the battle, the hills seemed to be covered in blood. Lillie, too, was interested in the old stories of the Lakota people and welcomed many of Chauncey's relatives into their home. After she died, the family found copies of legends in her handwriting, probably Chauncey's translations.[11]

Chauncey was a member of the Masonic order, and the Yellow Robe family was well known in Rapid City. A holiday insert in the 1915 *Rapid City Journal*, intended to attract businesses and investments, used a photograph of the Yellow Robes to publicize the city's identity. Chauncey seems to have been comfortable in the role of representative of educated Indians and proud of his accomplishments at Carlisle, which he attributed in a very personal way to Pratt's influence. Writing in 1920 on the occasion of Pratt's eightieth birthday, Chauncey told him, "I do not think there is any Carlisle man who is living today that is more indebted to you than I am. We have your photograph framed, hung upon our wall, and it is to me always a source of pleasure and comfort to look upon it. My life is your memorial."[12]

Later, in an autobiographical article, Chauncey wrote of Pratt, "Today, I owe to him and the inspiration I received from him all that I am."[13]

Nationally, Chauncey was active in the Society of American Indians, an organization of educated Native Americans devoted to progress and acculturation. He often spoke out against the exploitation of Indians and their history. In 1913, when he learned that Buffalo Bill Cody, the famous scout and Indian fighter, was appearing with General Nelson A. Miles in a film about the Wounded Knee massacre of 1890, he was incensed. The movie, being shot on the Pine Ridge Reservation, was planned to be so authentic that it would be filed among the historical archives of the War Department. Chauncey was outraged and spoke about it later at a meeting of the Society of American Indians in Albany, New York. He accused Cody and Miles of exploiting the event for their own glory. As reported in an Albany newspaper, Chauncey's words became bitter:

You ask how to settle the Indian troubles. . . . I have a suggestion. Let Buffalo Bill and General Miles take some soldiers and go around the reservations and shoot them down. That will settle his troubles. Let them do in earnest what they have been doing at the battlefield at Wounded Knee. These two, who were not even there when it happened, went back and became heroes for a moving picture machine. You laugh, but my heart does not laugh. Women and children and old men of my people, my relatives, were massacred with machine guns by soldiers of this Christian nation while the fighting men were away. That was bad – bad for the Sioux and bad for the White man. It was not a glorious battle, and I should think these two men would be glad they were not there; but no, they want to be heroes for moving pictures. You will be able to see their bravery and their hair-breadth escapes soon in your theaters.[14]

In a speech to the fourth annual conference of the Society of American Indians, held at Madison, Wisconsin, in October 1914, Chauncey repeated his condemnation:

A band of Sioux Indians, including women and children, unarmed, were massacred. The wounded were left to die without care at Wounded Knee by the United States troops just because they had founded a new religion called "The Indian Messiah."[15] This was a cowardly and criminal act without diplomacy. Twenty-three years afterward, the field of the Wounded Knee tragedy has been reproduced for historical preservation in moving picture films and called "The Last Great Battle of the Sioux." The whole production of the field was misrepresented and approved by the government. This is a disgrace and injustice to the Indian race. . . . I am not speaking here from selfish and sensitive motives, but from my own point of view, for cleaner civilization, education, and citizenship for my race. We are here today to consider the means to find a solution for our cause in this present generation, if it is ever settled. We have arrived at the point where it must be met. To the American Indian let there be given equal opportunities, equal responsibilities, equal education.[16]

Buffalo Bill Cody's Wild West Shows were extremely popular in the eastern states and Europe. Everyone wanted to see the warbonnets, tomahawks, and wild-riding warriors in action. The Indian performers, mostly Lakotas from Pine Ridge, reenacted Indian raids against stagecoaches to cheering audiences, performed dances, and demonstrated tribal customs. But Chauncey felt the same antipathy for these exhibitions as he did for the movie about Wounded Knee. He spoke of them at the October 1913 conference of the Society of American Indians in Denver, Colorado. "The Indian is not to be censured for the Wild West Show," he said, "for his condition and the present life which the Indian is forced to lead has drawn him into such shows. What benefit has the Indian derived from these Wild West Shows?" He added that the Indian Bureau had encouraged Indians to join these "fraudulent savage demonstrations before the world," degrading their traditions and "exhibiting the Indian worse than he ever was."[17]

Reacting to the news of Buffalo Bill's death in 1917, Chauncey wrote to Pratt: "So now 'Buffalo Bill' is dead and the supposed deeds he had claimed [are] all dead with him. He left nothing beneficial to humanity. A great deal of what he claimed to be was just enough hot air to fool the people and gain notoriety."[18]

In the 1920s, Chauncey was invited to appear on an early radio show broadcast from the South Dakota School of Mines in Rapid City. Station WCAT aired programs devoted to interviews with interesting people who made the Black Hills and Rapid City their home. At the start, Chauncey was somewhat nervous, but as the program progressed, he became more confident and related his boyhood memories of the time of Custer's defeat at the Little Bighorn and told the stories he had heard from warriors returning from the battle. Reminiscing about the way he had lived with his people before they were confined to reservations, he was suddenly overcome with emotion and exploded in a war whoop that literally knocked out the radio transmitter. The station went off the air with the war whoop resounding as the final message for the day.[19]

Chauncey sent his daughters to the Rapid City public schools because he wanted them to have the best possible preparation for modern society. Instead of the vocational courses in agriculture, blacksmithing, and domestic arts offered at the Indian school, he chose for them the more academic orientation of the one-room brick schoolhouse about a mile away. Rosebud enjoyed school very much and excelled there. She felt challenged by the material offered to the older students and sometimes tried to follow the lessons of the grades ahead of her. She developed a love of reading and was very pleased that the superintendent of the Indian school gave her access to his library.

Chauncey had one of the first cars in Rapid City, and Rosebud learned to drive it when she was fourteen. That same year an employee of the Indian school came to her father and asked for her hand in marriage. Chauncey, suddenly aware of his daughter's maturity, refused the offer. He had a long talk with her, Rosebud said, warning her that her good looks might attract unwanted attention. She was exceptionally attractive and throughout her life received compliments on her appearance. Della B. Vik, a local photographer, prevailed upon Chauncey to allow her to photograph Rosebud because of her beauty, but her father always accompanied her when she posed.[20]

Rosebud attended Rapid City High School, where she continued to excel and was a popular student. She developed a talent for the piano; in 1923, her father wrote proudly to Pratt that Rosebud "is a natural musician and has been now and then called upon to appear before the public."[21] In her senior year she was elected class treasurer. Then, in the fall of 1925, she went off to Vermillion to attend the University of South Dakota. At the railroad station amid final goodbyes, she remembered her father saying, "Rosebud, if you were my son, you would be going to West Point."

Chauncey's observations and experience had convinced him that the majority of whites were totally ignorant of what Indians were capable of achieving. He instilled in Rosebud the idea that it was the Indians' responsibility to prove their abilities and to participate fully in all aspects of American life. Rosebud followed her father's philosophy throughout her life. He, along with other well-known members of the Society of American Indians, were lobbying the federal government to grant Indians United States citizenship. Through the efforts of that organization and others, citizenship was finally granted to all Indians when Rosebud was a senior in high school, on June 2, 1924.

Despite the state's large Indian population, Rosebud was one of only two Indians enrolled at the University of South Dakota. For the first time, she could understand the feelings of homesickness her father had felt at Carlisle when he said that he had looked toward the western sky and cried within his heart for his parents and the free life he had led. Chauncey answered Rosebud's letter about her homesickness by reminding her how much better prepared she was academically, socially, and culturally than he had been. He assured her that once she became acclimated to college life and began to participate in its many activities, she would make friends and begin to enjoy herself.

Every year the university held a beauty contest called "Vanity Fair." The residents of each campus housing unit submitted a picture of the girl they thought could win the contest, and the winners' pictures were published in the yearbook, *The Coyote*. Rosebud did not remember who asked her for a photograph to give to the judges, but she remembered that she represented Dakota Hall and remarked how ironic it was that she was the only real Dakota living in Dakota Hall.[22] That year the contest organizers decided to ask a Hollywood judge to select the winner. Sixteen photographs, without names or other identifications, were sent to Cecil B. DeMille, the film producer and director. According to newspaper accounts, Rosebud caused a sensation when, after the judging, it was learned that she was a Sioux Indian and a relative of Sitting Bull. As Rosebud said, "I came in fourth or fifth, but the fact that I was an Indian caused a lot of excitement." The story in the university newspaper was picked up by the national wire services, and when DeMille realized that he had chosen an Indian, he offered Rosebud the leading role in *Ramona*, his film about Indians. But Chauncey was afraid of Hollywood's reputation and would not hear of it. At the same time, the Shubert organization, prominent New York producers, saw the articles written about DeMille's "find" and offered Rosebud a walk-on part in Eddie Cantor's Broadway show *Whoopee*. She reluctantly declined.

The publicity about Rosebud was generated by Ed Morrow, also a student at the university, who worked as a reporter both for the student newspaper and for the *Sioux Falls Press*. His ancestry was African American, and he seems to have been drawn to Rosebud as a Native. When he first met her in an English class, he regarded her as charming, bright, slightly distant, and having "a royal attitude." She was, he thought, something like Audrey Hepburn – slender, charming, and above the rest of the crowd. To him, Rosebud was more cultured than the other female students, and he believed that many of them resented the attention she received. Ed became Rosebud's devoted admirer, dubbing the two of them "the Noble

Savages," and did everything he could to make sure that publicity about her participation in campus events reached the local and national newspapers.[23]

Ed especially remembered the Stroller Talent Competitions, all-campus student entertainment productions. Rosebud entered the competition in 1926. Enlisting the help of another female student from Dakota Hall, a non-Indian, she decided to put on a program of Lakota dances. Dressed in male attire, she performed the hoop dance, the rabbit dance (a couple's dance with her friend) and the war dance. Graceful and proud, Rosebud left no doubt among the audience that the dances were authentic.[24] She won first prize, fifty dollars, and more publicity for – as one of Morrow's articles in the *Sioux Falls Press* put it – "the most beautiful Indian girl in America."

Rosebud reported only one experience of prejudice at the university. After having rushed a sorority and been assured that she would be admitted, at the last minute she was told publicly that the bylaws explicitly banned non-Caucasian members.

Rosebud's schooling was put on hold when she was called home to Rapid City because her mother was gravely ill. She stayed with her mother until her death on April 6, 1927. Lillie was only forty-two years old. Informing Lillie's friend Clara of his wife's death, Chauncey wrote, "She was in her prime of life, a beautiful womanhood when she died. We cannot ever forget her as a mother and wife, but we cannot question the wisdom of God, why she was called away from this world." In a second letter he added, "Sometimes it doesn't seem possible that Lillie is gone."[25]

In the midst of the family's grief over Lillie's death, Chauncey was called upon to organize an event on behalf of the Lakota people. President Calvin A. Coolidge was to come to the Black Hills for about three months, from the middle of June until the end of the first week in September. On August 4 he and Mrs. Coolidge were to attend the annual Days of '76 celebration in Deadwood, South Dakota. During this pageant the president was to be made an honorary member of the Sioux tribe in recognition of his role in granting citizenship to the Indians in 1924.

Chauncey threw himself into preparations for the Coolidge ceremony. For weeks every spare hour was taken up by conferring with the chiefs, listening to the advice, suggestions, and complaints of the many committees, and choosing a suitable Indian name for the president.

The induction ceremonies were held in the natural amphitheater at Deadwood, with Chief Henry Standing Bear and others taking part in the ceremony as Chauncey conferred upon President Coolidge the name Leading Eagle (*Waŋblí Thokáhe*, First Eagle). Rosebud placed on Coolidge's head a magnificent double-trail eagle feather warbonnet, truly worthy of the impressive occasion.[26]

After a ceremonial chant, accompanied by the beating of drums, Chauncey stepped forward and, placing both hands on the president's shoulders, said earnestly in Lakota, "Today, Mr. President, you are a one hundred per cent American by adoption into an aboriginal tribe. Good White Father, we welcome you into our tribe. We hope you will continue to guide this great nation on to a still greater destiny."[27] He continued in English:

It is the greatest honor to the Sioux Tribe of South Dakota to bestow upon you the emblem of the Sioux Nation in a war bonnet, and to welcome you to our tribe. We name you Leading Eagle, Wamblee-Tokaha. By this name you are to be known – King and the greatest chief, which is signified by the bonnet and the name you bear. I congratulate you in the name of the Sioux Nation, and express the hope that you will continue to guide the will of this Nation to its great destiny.[28]

Coolidge was the first and only president of the United States to have this honor conferred upon him by the Sioux Nation.

4

New York

Shortly after the Coolidge ceremony in the summer of 1927, Rosebud took the famous Twentieth Century Limited train to New York, eager to pursue a theatrical career. Before she left the University of South Dakota to be with her ailing mother, one of her teachers, a woman, had offered to serve as chaperone for Rosebud on her first trip to New York. She knew a theatrical manager, Arthur de Cinq Mars, whose professional name was Arthur Seymour, and put Rosebud in touch with him. The two began an intensive correspondence.

Chauncey thought that with a college teacher as chaperone, Rosebud would be far safer in New York than in Hollywood. As it turned out, the teacher was planning to leave her husband in South Dakota with the idea of returning to her previous life as an actress. She did not accompany Rosebud on the train trip to New York but did meet her upon her arrival.

Until then, Rosebud's longest train trips had been with her family to visit her grandparents in Tacoma, Washington, but this time she was alone and frightened. She felt that she was being stared at because of the recent Coolidge publicity, but no one spoke to her about it. There was a mix-up with the train tickets from Rapid City to Chicago, and Rosebud recalled a gentleman named Captain Lord, who, "seeing that there was no berth available for me, gave me his own. I have never forgotten his kindness to me in an awkward situation."

Arthur Seymour had arranged for rooms at the Westbury Hotel for Rosebud and her chaperone, and on Rosebud's first night in New York he took her to the Roxy Theater. She greatly enjoyed the feature and the stage show, but the newsreel proved to be the highlight of the evening: there Rosebud saw herself on screen, putting the feathered warbonnet on President Coolidge's head! Afterward, they had a Chinese dinner, and Rosebud became violently ill. She was never sure whether it was the food or the excitement of seeing herself at the Roxy.

Since her teacher had seen Rosebud in the Strollers Talent Competition at the University of South Dakota, she proposed that Rosebud develop an Indian dance act. With Seymour as her manager, Rosebud appeared on stages in hotels and theaters and was very popular, many in her audiences recognizing her from the newsreel and newspaper coverage. For her night-club act she wore a stylized American Indian costume. On one occasion, at the Hotel Pennsylvania, an overenthusiastic patron who had had too much to drink started to pull at her clothing. Without missing a beat, Rosebud tapped him on the head with her tomahawk. He fainted and had to be carried out. The next day she received a dozen yellow roses with a note of apology from her inebriated admirer.

Arthur Seymour was a handsome and sophisticated New Yorker. Although he was twenty-five years older than Rosebud, the two of them fell in love, and within the year they married. In 1929 they had a daughter, Rosebud Tachcawin de Cinq Mars.[1] That was the year of the stock market crash and the beginning of the Great Depression. Arthur had been well off – even owned a sailboat named *Act Four* – but within a few weeks, like many others, he had lost virtually everything.

Now, at the age of twenty-one, with an infant daughter, Rosebud needed to help out financially. Her husband engaged Stephen Briggs, a manager, to handle Rosebud's bookings, and he began to schedule public presentations for her. Clyde Fisher, who was at that time an assistant curator in the Department of Public Education at the American Museum of Natural History, invited her to speak at the museum. She was an instant success, telling not only Lakota myths and legends but also stories from the Eastern Woodland tribes, which she learned from books in the museum library. Rosebud felt strongly that people living on the East Coast should know something about the original inhabitants of the area. For these appearances she wore a family heirloom, a magnificent beaded deerskin dress made early in the twentieth century by women of her father's family. Its unusual overall design depicted the many war exploits of Iron Plume, her father's uncle.[2]

Luckily, a friend of the Yellow Robe family was already living in New York when Rosebud arrived. Edith Daub, who had been a YMCA representative years before, had gone west on annual visits to YMCA organizations in each of the Indian schools in South Dakota. When Rosebud came to New York, Daub became an important link to home, and they maintained a warm relationship for many years.

After Lillie's death, Chauncey found it impossible to continue at the Rapid City Indian School. In the spring of 1928 he took a leave of absence and, with his youngest daughter, Evelyn, left for New York City to visit Rosebud. Chauncina arrived in New York from South Dakota shortly thereafter.

Shortly after his arrival, on a Sunday afternoon visit to the American Museum of Natural History, Chauncey was recognized by a young Penobscot woman named Molly Spotted Elk. She, too, had come to New York seeking a theatrical career.[3] Molly had just signed a contract with Douglas Burden and William Chandler for a leading role in a movie they were about to produce called *The Silent Enemy*. Most of the cast members, all of whom were Indians, had already been selected, but Burden was having great difficulty finding the right person for the role of Chetoga, the chief. The minute he saw Chauncey, he exclaimed, "There, that's the man I want; he's perfect for the part."

Burden immediately offered him the role of the chief in the movie, but Chauncey refused. He had always denounced Wild West shows, exhibitions, and motion pictures that commercialized and demeaned the Indian, and he assumed that *The Silent Enemy* would be yet another such disgraceful portrayal. Burden failed to convince Chauncey that he intended this picture to present a truthful portrayal of Native American life before the coming of the whites.

During this visit to New York, Chauncey was lunching one day with Irvin S. Cobb, the humorist. A friend of Cobb's approached their table and after being introduced, the man placed an Indian-head nickel on the table. "Is this your good friend?" he asked. The resemblance between Chauncey's profile and that on the coin was striking. "No," said Chauncey quietly with a twinkle in his eyes, "I am waiting to be put on the ten-dollar gold piece."

In New York during the 1920s, Sunday night receptions at the homes of prominent members of society were important gauges of social standing. The Sunday nights at the home of Edward Deming – an artist of Indian and western life who, with his wife, became well known for a series of illustrated children's books depicting a variety of American Indian peoples – brought together large and diverse groups that included explorers, naturalists, and businessmen. Deming's biographer, Thomas Lamb, reported that Chauncey was a frequent guest:

One evening as Yellow Robe listened to Deming speaking of the Indians to another friend, Yellow Robe turned to the friend and said, "He is telling me things about my own people that even I did not know."

On another occasion, a businessman attempted to converse with Yellow Robe, using pidgin English, to which the Red Man replied in grunts. As the misguided businessman was leaving, Yellow Robe turned to Deming and said, "Who does he think Indians are?"[4]

Rosebud recalled fondly the special Sunday nights at the Demings, to which she, Chauncina, and Evelyn accompanied their father.[5]

After visiting Rosebud for a few weeks, Chauncey returned to Rapid City, leaving Evelyn, now age seven, in Rosebud and Arthur's care. Chauncina also remained in New York.

Chauncey was keenly interested in politics and was being considered as the Republican nominee for Congress from South Dakota's Third District. He was very pleased at this proposal but was too modest to consider it a personal honor. He looked upon it as evidence that the Indian was becoming as integral a part of the American nation as the white. He said, "If I am nominated for congress, I will not look upon my candidacy as that of an Indian, but rather as that of an American citizen, exercising the rights of a citizen of the republic, not only of franchise but of running for office."[6] In Rapid City in the summer of 1928, Chauncey wrote to the *Hot Springs Star* in response to an item that said, "If he [Chauncey] goes to New York, he probably will never go to congress from South Dakota." In reply, Chauncey noted that he had been urged to run for Congress in the last congressional campaign, but since he was then in the civil service, he was not allowed to engage in political activity. He had since retired, however: "I choose to run for congress from South Dakota in two years from now. My going to New York or any other cause should not bar my citizenship of South Dakota."[7] But Chauncey would die before those two years were up.

Meanwhile, Burden had refused to give up on persuading Chauncey to take a role in *The Silent Enemy*. He called Rosebud and convinced her of the sincerity of his intention to produce an authentic depiction of Indian life. She in turn wrote to her father urging him to reconsider Burden's offer and suggested that this was his opportunity to help achieve a better understanding between Indians and whites. In the end, she persuaded him to return to New York to play the role of the chief and to serve as technical director. While the film was in production, his image appeared on the cover of *Collier's National Weekly* for March 2, 1929.

It took almost a year of hard and tedious work, including a frigid winter under extremely difficult conditions at Lake Temagami, Ontario, for the film to be completed.[8] The "silent enemy" was hunger, and Long Lance, who played the leading role, told Rosebud how conscientiously Chauncey did his work. Wanting to make the scene of Chief Chetoga's death by starvation as realistic as possible, Chauncey fasted for almost two weeks before the scene was shot.[9]

This silent film was made on the cusp of the transition to talkies. After filming was completed, the producers decided to insert a prologue, written *and* spoken by Chauncey.[10] Rosebud commented later that she had never been aware that her father spoke English with a Lakota accent until she heard the movie prologue. He was such a dynamic speaker, though, that his heavily Lakota-accented English did not seem to distract his listeners.

The Silent Enemy opened at the Criterion Theater on Broadway on May 5, 1930. It was acclaimed by the critics as one of the greatest Indian pictures ever produced.

Unfortunately, during his stay in New York to record the prologue, Chauncey contracted pneumonia and was hospitalized at the Rockefeller Institute in New York. Although he was well cared for, he seemed to have lost his will to live. He died on the third anniversary of his wife's death, April 6, 1930, and was buried according to Masonic rites beside her in the Mountain View Cemetery in Rapid City.

After Chauncey's death, President Coolidge, remembering the summer of 1927 during which he had come to know Chauncey at the Rapid City Indian School, wrote that he had been "very much impressed with the dignified manner in which Chief Yellow Robe conducted the school and the fine appearance made by the pupils. It was easy to see that he was a dominating influence, which inspired all his surroundings." Referring to the ceremony in which he was adopted into the tribe, Coolidge reminisced:

No one could have witnessed the granting of this token of friendship and brother-hood without appreciating the spiritual significance, which Chief Yellow Robe gave to it. He wished to confer on me, as a representative of the Government of the United States, everything that he felt was good and worth preserving in the Indian life for the same reason that he constantly strove to teach his people to acquire and benefit by all that he believed was good and worthy in the life of the White people.

Coolidge concluded his tribute to Chauncey: "He was a born leader who realized that the destiny of the Indian is indissolubly bound up with the destiny of our country. His loyalty to his tribe and people made him a most patriotic American."[11]

5

Jones Beach

Soon after her father's death the opportunity arose that brought Rosebud to Jones Beach. The Long Island State Park Commission was building a network of parkways through private lands on Long Island to provide access to the new Jones Beach State Park, which opened on August 4, 1929. The project was controversial, however, and as a public relations gesture the commission sponsored a series of public lectures during 1929–30, offered without charge, to schools, communities, fraternal organizations, and women's clubs all over New York but particularly on Long Island. Two speakers were chosen: Rosebud, and the director of the Long Island Bird Sanctuary, who usually appeared together. They spoke about their own specialties, and their presentations proved to be very popular.[1]

In contrast to Coney Island, Jones Beach banned carnival attractions; the park was designed to focus on the beach itself. The elegant architecture of its central pavilion and two bathhouses was reminiscent of the French Riviera. In 1930 Rosebud was hired at the new park as an instructor at the archery range, the assumption being that, as an Indian, she would be familiar with bows and arrows. She admitted she didn't know much about target shooting, but she learned quickly. "I realized that most visitors to the beach were archery novices," she told me, "and I just showed them where to stand and how to aim for the target." The original bows were made of wood – costly Alex Taylor equipment with a strength of twenty to twenty-five pounds – and were of high quality, but they proved inappropriate for the humid beach conditions. At Rosebud's suggestion they were replaced with metal alloy bows, which would not warp.

The archery range became a center of attention. Local newspapers played up the novelty. One headline proclaimed, "Daughter of Sioux Chieftain Attracts Thousands to State Park Archery Range." The tone of the article matched the headline: "As straight as the arrows she shoots from her bow, Miss Rosebud Yellow Robe attracts the attention of the thousands of people who each weekend and throughout the week stop to watch the archery range at the Jones Beach State Park, where this comely . . . Indian girl teaches archery."[2] As the newspaper went on to recount, Rosebud had also started storytelling sessions. In her beaded deerskin dress, with her long hair neatly braided, she fascinated children and adults alike who came to hear her tell traditional Indian stories, many of which she had learned from her father. She had also prepared by reading tales of the local Long Island tribes at the American Museum of Natural History the winter before.

The story hours proved very popular, and soon Rosebud was presenting them at scheduled times both during the week and on weekends. She divided the children by age into two groups, the younger called Eaglets and the older Little Eagles. Toward the end of the summer of 1932, just before the reopening of school, she staged a ceremony characterized as a "peace council fire" that was attended by a crowd estimated at one thousand people, including more than three hundred children.[3]

When park administrators, reacting to her popularity, asked Rosebud to develop the Indian program further, she suggested establishing a Plains Indian village for children where she could tell stories, teach crafts, and supervise other activities all day long throughout the summer.[4] Continuing publicity during the winter attracted even greater numbers of children to the Jones Beach Indian Village the following summer, when three tipis were placed on a large, grassy lawn. Rosebud designated the largest the Council Tipi, which contained museum cases that exhibited artifacts borrowed from the American Museum of Natural History. The other two tipis would serve as clubhouses for the Eaglets and Little Eagles.[5]

Rosebud understood that most of the children would know very little about Indians, and she wanted to introduce them to the diversity of tribes in North America. To that end, the exhibits in the Council Tipi were rotated to display at different times material representing a variety of culture areas. Storytelling then included tales from the tribe featured in the current exhibit, though Rosebud commented that stories of the Lakotas and the Eastern Woodlands tribes were the most popular.

Mabel Powers, an Iroquois elder whom she met through Clyde Fisher at the American Museum of Natural History, shared some of her people's stories with Rosebud for her use at the Indian Village.[6] "Gray Rabbit Sings for Snow," one of those Eastern Woodlands stories, became a perennial favorite with the children, many of whom returned time and again to hear it. It was certainly my favorite story, and when I close my eyes, I can see and hear Rosebud telling it:

Gray Rabbit was very handsome. Like all the gray rabbits in his family, he had a long fluffy tail almost like a squirrel's tail. Sometimes when he was walking along the river he would come to a quiet pool where he could see a reflection of himself. He always held up his gray fluffy tail and waved it back and forth while admiring himself. Gray Rabbit was disappointed. The month of white snow had arrived but no snow had come. Gray Rabbit thought about the snow; he loved to play in it, and winter was no fun without snow. Suddenly he thought about the Medicine Man. He knew that the Medicine Man could do almost anything. Off he went to find him.

He entered Medicine Man's lodge quietly and then sat down beside him after they had greeted each other. "My friend, what may I do for you?" asked the Medicine Man. Rabbit told him his great wish for snow. The Medicine Man said, "If you will learn the song I will teach you and go back into the woods and sing it, it will snow.

Rabbit listened carefully to the words and the tune as Medicine Man sang. After he had memorized the song he thanked him and hurried back to the deep woods.

He began to sing, "Ah ga na ha hey, ah ga na ha hey da ton hey hey hey hey hey hey," which meant, Snow, snow, how I wish it would snow.

The strangest thing happened – it began to snow. When Rabbit sang lightly, the snow fell lightly; when he sang loudly, the snow fell heavily. Rabbit wanted a lot of snow so he sang "Ah ga na ha hey" at the top of his voice. Soon the ground was all white and the trees were all white and Gray Rabbit ran, rolled, jumped, and slid in the snow.

Rabbit had lost his voice. He was so hoarse he could not sing, and the snow stopped falling. He was very tired. He looked around for a place to spend the night. He saw what he thought was a small bush sticking out of the snow. So he crawled into a crotch of the branches, closed his eyes, and was soon fast asleep.

That night a warm rain began to fall, and as it hit the snow it began to melt away. All night the warm rain fell. Gray Rabbit was so tired he did not feel it.

The next morning when Rabbit opened his eyes, there he was in the tip-top branches of a willow tree. The ground was far below him.

Rabbit was not a bird, he could not fly out of the tree. He was not a squirrel, he couldn't climb down. He realized there was only one way to get down and that was to jump.

Arrival at Carlisle Indian School, 1883. *Left to right:* Richard Yellow Robe, Henry Standing Bear, and Chauncey Yellow Robe. BS-CH-16. Courtesy Cumberland County Historical Society, Carlisle PA.

Chauncey Yellow Robe at Carlisle Indian School, c. 1890. PA-CH2-20. Courtesy Cumberland County Historical Society, Carlisle PA.

Chauncey and his father, Yellow Robe, upon Chauncey's return from the Carlisle Indian School, 1895. Author's collection.

Wedding photograph of Chauncey Yellow Robe and Lillian Springer, May 22, 1906.
Courtesy Minnilusa Pioneer Museum/Journey Museum, Rapid City SD.

Rosebud Yellow Robe at age five, 1912, with a teddy bear. Author's collection.

Rosebud Yellow Robe at age seven, 1914, reading a book. Her beaded and fringed deerskin dress and leggings were handmade for her. Author's collection.

The Yellow Robe family in 1915 (*left to right:* Rosebud, Lillie, Chauncina, Chauncey), as they appeared in Holiday Greetings from the *Rapid City Journal.* Rapid City (SD) Public Library. Courtesy *Rapid City Journal.*

Calvin Coolidge, Rosebud Yellow Robe, Chauncey Yellow Robe at the president's induction into the Lakota tribe, 1927. Author's collection.

Professional photograph of Rosebud Yellow Robe during her University years, 1925–26.
She wears a beaded headband with feather, traditional Lakota dress and leggings of
fringed deerskin, and beaded moccasins; she is holding beaded pipe and flint bags.
Courtesy University of South Dakota Foundation.

Overview of Jones Beach Indian Village, 1934. Courtesy New York Office of Parks, Recreation and Historic Preservation.

Rosebud Yellow Robe with children around campfire at Jones Beach Indian Village, July 6, 1934. Courtesy New York Office of Parks, Recreation and Historic Preservation.

Story hour with Rosebud Yellow Robe (*center*) at Jones Beach Indian Village, 1934. Courtesy New York Office of Parks, Recreation and Historic Preservation.

Rosebud Yellow Robe, 1985, photo taken in preparation for painted portrait. Photo by Ann McCory. Author's collection.

He was brave but he decided to close his eyes before he jumped, and as he jumped he felt something tear. He was so excited he had forgotten to lift his rain-soaked tail. It caught in the crotch of the branch and tore off so it was only a short stump of a tail. He landed on the ground on his face and a sharp rock cut his upper lip in two.

Ever since then all the gray rabbits have split upper lips and short tails.

And if you go out into the woods in the springtime, you will see the willow trees are covered with gray rabbits' tails that have shrunk in the rain.

If it is a gray cloudy day during the winter and you are bored, try singing the Rabbit song. It's a magical song – perhaps it will snow![7]

Rosebud was concerned that the children's first impressions of American Indians be positive ones. She told a *New York Times* reporter: "They must not begin to think of Indians as scalp-lifting savages. When I say, 'Let's play Indian' to a group of three or four hundred children, it means there will be story telling, singing and dancing. We shall play the skunk game and the rabbit game and the game of the fox and the four winds and many others."[8]

Over the years the Jones Beach administration added facilities as necessary at the Indian Village – including a well-built wooden structure called the craft building – activities there became a dependable routine. A mimeographed brochure from 1947 announced the daily schedule and provided information for participants:

12:00 noon	Handicraft classes
2:00	Songs and Stories
3:00	Turtle Races
3:30	Indian games
4:15	Handicraft classes
5:45	Craft materials, "Put Away songs," Stories, games and dances

No handicraft on Sundays or holidays.

Instruction in weaving, beadwork, basketry, carving, pottery, leathercraft, metalcraft, finger painting and in the making of Tom-Toms, rattles and war bonnets.

Under the direction of Rosebud Yellow Robe

Handicraft classes are open to all boys and girls 8 years of age.

All classes are open to adults.

Material and instructions are free to all.

There will be no instruction in basketry on Mondays, nor beadwork on Fridays. However, advanced pupils in both crafts may work on projects already started, with special permission.

Special Events will be posted on the bulletin board.

All activities are subject to change without notice.

Children and Adults using the facilities at the Indian Village do so at their own risk.

Chairs on the lawn are for the use of parents of children coming to the Indian Village.

HOW TO JOIN HANDICRAFT CLASSES

1. Register at workshop and sign file.
2. State on card what crafts you wish to study.
3. Materials and equipment will be furnished to you to work with but must be returned for storage at the end of each session.
4. Your name will be placed on unfinished work and kept for you until you come to the Indian Village again, but if you do not return within two weeks, your work may be given to someone else to complete.
5. All finished work becomes your property, but if requested, you must leave same to be displayed at the Closing Exhibit. Articles kept for exhibit will be mailed to you if you cannot call for same personally.

Attendance prizes are awarded at the Closing Campfire. To qualify for same, you must sign the Daily Attendance Sheet each time you come to the Indian Village.[9]

Reaching back into my memories of summers spent at Jones Beach Indian Village is very much like unfolding a map into the past. One must picture life before television, air-conditioning, family vacations at Disney World, computers and computer games, and cell phones. Life moved at a slower pace, centered on family and close neighborhood connections. Saturday trips to the movies were the height of excitement. Listening to the adventures of the Lone Ranger and Tonto on the radio provided most of what children knew about American Indians.

At the Indian Village, however, there was a sense that everything about you was real: this was how Indians lived and conducted themselves. Rosebud wanted it to be a place where children and adults alike could learn something true about Indians, hear stories, work on crafts, and participate in games and other activities. While we were busy at the Indian Village, we felt secure in the belief that we were learning things that were authentic, important, and interesting on a subject that few others knew anything about. Back at school we had something unique to share with our teachers and schoolmates.

The car ride to Jones Beach was part of the enjoyment. Once we had parked in Parking Field 4, the excitement grew. We never knew exactly what to expect. Rosebud had a set routine, but the sequence varied. It was comforting to know that there would always be storytelling and craft work, the making of something unique that would become a feature of "Show and Tell" for school next fall. Rosebud was often assisted by an attractive young woman we called Buddy. Only later did I learn that Buddy was Rosebud's daughter. Rosebud's younger sister Evelyn also assisted her at times with craft instruction, though she chose to wear the nautical uniform of Jones Beach employees rather than Indian dress.

Handicrafts included weaving, carving, pottery, leathercraft, metalcraft, fingerpainting, and the making of drums and rattles. We made baskets, carefully wetting the materials so that they could be woven easily and adding raffia strips to make them more colorful. We used bead looms to make bracelets and the bands we needed for our feathered warbonnets. I remember that making a warbonnet turned into a family project. After cutting the crown of a used hat (my Dad's), we sewed the beaded band to the front and attached the covered end of each individual feather to the hat. At the back we added a long "trail," a piece of material to which we also attached feathers. It was a time-consuming and intricate process that took many visits to complete. A photo of Rosebud and my family around a large table covered with all the materials needed to make a double-trail warbonnet recalls one of my favorite memories of summers at the Indian Village.

The turtle races at the Indian Village always resulted in crowds of adults watching from the boardwalk. The turtles lived in a pen near the craft building, where we could feed and water them. Each turtle had a number painted on its back, and each of us had a favorite. They were placed carefully in a special circular raceway with partitioned spaces for four to six turtles. The turtle that reached the outer frame first was the winner. We children yelled, jumped up and down, and had fun cheering our favorites on to victory. Not until years later did I realize that some of the adults on the boardwalk were there to bet on a favorite turtle to win.

Council Fires – special Wednesday events – and shadow plays spread excitement throughout the summer. There was a shadow play at the end of the season as a farewell celebration. The one I remember participating in was *The Song of Hiawatha*, repeated on two nights. Longfellow's poem was acted out, with the principal characters, human and animal, seen on a huge screen behind which were real and constructed figures. Rosebud read the script, and all the actors moved or manipulated their props in accordance with her cues. The performances were given on the great lawn at night, lights shining from behind the screen to cast the shadows. It was very exciting! We all stayed up well past our bedtimes. After all, we didn't have to go to school the next morning. And this was before air-conditioning; it was delightfully cool at the beach and hot and uncomfortable at home. My parents were happy to stay until quite late to keep cool for as long as possible.

When I think back to my own days as a child at the Indian Village, I realize how remarkably free it was of disciplinary problems. I don't remember Rosebud or her helpers ever admonishing a visitor to the village. Those who were noisy were given icy stares by the other children and by adults in the audience and soon quieted down or left. All the craft materials were free, and during craft lessons we were busy trying to finish our projects. If we did not finish, we could leave them for the next day. Skill and completing a previous project seemed to be the main criteria for being permitted to start a new one. Theft was not a significant issue, perhaps because of the way the state park was run and the village's generosity with materials. We seemed to know that this was a special time, doing something out of the ordinary with someone who was willing to teach us skills few on Long Island had. We were learning how to be like Indians, and we loved it. I can remember working on a project all day for several days at a time, stopping only to receive instruction, listen to a story, or eat a meal. Although different children might attend from day to day, during the course of a week a group of regulars would show up. By the end of summer we had become fast friends. It was a joy to be part of a group of children all interested in the same things and having the help of an expert while learning worthwhile skills.

During her years at Jones Beach, Rosebud also appeared on *Aunt Susan*, a CBS radio children's program. Shirley Plume, who was married to Rosebud's cousin Paul Plume, told me that one day in the 1930s while she was helping to fix breakfast for her family at their home on the Pine Ridge Reservation, she heard Rosebud's delightfully distinctive voice in the next room. "How can that be?" she thought. "Rosebud is in New York." Then she heard Rosebud telling the story with which her father had many times enthralled audiences. Chauncey would declare that the American Indians were God's chosen people, and furthermore, he could prove it:

In the days of creation, God took some clay and began to shape Man. When he was satisfied with the shape of the clay figure, he put it into the oven to fire. He had so much on his mind that he left the figure in the oven too long and out came the Black Man. He decided to try again. Once more he molded the clay, and once more he was satisfied with his work. He placed the figure into the oven. This time he removed his creation too early, for this Man was too pale and underbaked, and the White Man was created. Always striving for perfection, God once again shaped the clay into his image and fired it in the oven. This time, he waited just a little longer. . . . Now here was a Man who was exactly the right color, just glowing with God's perfection, and the Red race was created, God's finest achievement![10]

In 1937, Alfred Frantz contacted Rosebud. A fellow student from her days at the University of South Dakota, he was employed in public relations and had been hired to publicize the maiden voyage of the *Oslofjord*, a new ship of the Norwegian American Line, by orchestrating a suitable publicity event to welcome its first landing in New York. When a friend asked facetiously, "Why don't you get a bunch of Indians?" he thought of Rosebud. Although he did not know her personally, he had often seen her in Vermillion, and he knew that she was in New York. He found her name in the telephone directory and called to offer her the job. Rosebud accepted. She was to appear in Indian dress and bring a gift of peace to present to a Norwegian representative dressed as a Viking. The welcome for the *Oslofjord* went off well, and the event attracted news coverage not only in the New York City press but even in *Life* magazine. And a story in *Time* featured the fact that Rosebud had lost her peace pipe at the ceremony. It turned out that the Viking had walked off with it, assuming that, like the moccasins she had presented to him, it was intended as a gift.[11]

Throughout the World War II years, activities at Jones Beach were curtailed. Rosebud contributed to the war effort by working for the Sperry Gyroscope Company in Lake Success, Long Island, founded in 1910 by engineer and inventor Elmer Ambrose Sperry. The company manufactured devices used in nautical and aviation navigation and stabilization. Rosebud tested gyroscopes and became expert in checking bombsights.

At war's end, however, Rosebud returned to the Indian Village and continued to direct it until 1950. There, thousands of children and adults alike believed that they had met "a real Indian princess." Despite Rosebud's protestations that there never was such a person, to her devoted followers she would always be a princess.

6

Later Years

In the years after Rosebud left the Indian Village at Jones Beach, she worked part time as a doctor's receptionist in Forest Hills, New York, the town in which she and her family lived. She was also an active member of St. Luke's Episcopal Church. Rosebud maintained a clear boundary between her private and professional worlds. Few knew of her family, her responsibilities, and her myriad outside interests. Professionally, she was identified as Miss Yellow Robe.

Rosebud and her husband Arthur had raised Rosebud's younger sister Evelyn along with their own daughter, whom the family called both Buddy and Taki – from her Indian name, Tachcawin (Deer Woman). Evelyn excelled as a student, attended Bayside High School, and became the first female president of Arista, the New York City high school honor society. She then went to Mount Holyoke College, supported by a scholarship provided with the help of Ruth Muskrat Bronson at the Bureau of Indian Affairs. Buddy remained in New York, trained in art, and won awards in Indian art competitions. For a time before her marriage, Chauncina, the middle Yellow Robe sister, also lived with Rosebud and Arthur. In 1951, Arthur died, and Rosebud married Alfred Frantz, who had become a close family friend. When Buddy's husband died, Rosebud's granddaughter Karen was only four years old, and Rosebud took on the responsibility of helping to raise her. And for me, too, she became a second mother. To all of us she gave her greatest gift, unconditional love and support.

Rosebud continued to present frequent lectures and storytelling sessions at schools and civic organizations throughout the New York area, and at the American Museum of Natural History and the Donnell Library (part of the New York City public library system), as well. The warmth of her personality appealed to audiences of adults and children alike. She also made personalized records for children, each with a message to the child for whom it was made, followed by a telling of one of her father's stories.[1]

In 1951 Rosebud was hired by Twentieth-Century Fox to undertake a national publicity tour for the movie, *Broken Arrow*. The film told the story of a peace pact between the Apaches and the United States in 1870. The broken arrow symbolized peace, and the message of the film was the need for mutual understanding as the basis for better relations between Indians and whites.[2] Rosebud was hopeful that the movie might have a beneficial effect: "It is a wonderful portrayal of relationships between the White man and the red man years ago. I hope it will bring about a better understanding."[3]

In a newspaper interview that year, headlined "This Indian Princess Says There's No Such Thing as an Indian Princess," the writer commented that Rosebud had scratched out the word "Princess" before her name saying, "I wish they wouldn't do this to me! There is no such thing as an Indian princess. It all started when Pocahontas went to England and the English named her 'Lady Rebecca.' The Americans decided that she must be royalty, so they made her 'Princess.' It's an old English, rather than an old Indian custom."[4]

In another interview that same year a newspaper headline read, "Rosebud Yellow Robe Says 'Pfui' to 'Ugh' as Indian Word." Rosebud voiced many complaints about the portrayal of Indians on radio, screen, and television, but her greatest complaint was the word "Ugh": "That horrid word! Why is it everyone expects Indians to says 'Ugh!' in the movies. They can speak perfectly good English. Still they are forced to use bad English and utter guttural syllables because the producers seem to think that adds color. The number of authentic Indian movies which have been made could be counted on the fingers of one hand," she said. "In all the rest, Indians are screaming, scalping villains. That simply is not true to life. And with all the Indian movies being put on television, a new generation of children are learning the old stereotypes about whooping, warring Indians, as if there weren't anything else interesting about us."[5]

In her later years Rosebud made a point of *not* wearing her Indian garb for public presentations. She said, "I *am* Indian. It doesn't depend on what I wear." Still, she would always take her heaviest beaded dress with her when she spoke to an audience and, as part of her lecture, she would invite them to guess its weight (eighteen pounds).

Proud of her heritage and her accomplishments, Rosebud wanted others to know how meaningful her Indian identity was to her and to understand that Indians could succeed in the modern world. When the Coordinating Committee on American Indian Affairs met in New York in October 1948, Rosebud participated as representative of the National Congress of American Indians.[6] Following in her father's footsteps, she remained interested and active in Indian causes throughout her life, speaking out against prejudice and injustice. In a television interview she again complained of the portrayal of Indians in western films. Movies and television shows that presented Indians as villains, she insisted, were powerful forces shaping children's impressions. "These days," Rosebud commented in a 1951 interview, "when even tiny children hear that I am an Indian, they retreat from me."[7] In that same interview she spoke of social inequities and of American Indian land problems. She was keenly aware of the post–World War II congressional policy that threatened for a time to terminate the federal relationship with tribes and abolish Indian reservations. Her home on Long Island was a hub of activity for the area's Indian community.

Rosebud published two books designed to introduce children to Indian culture. *An Album of the American Indian* (1969) gives an overview of Native life from earliest times to the present and includes several pictures of Rosebud's family. *Tonweya and the Eagles* (1979) is a retelling of Lakota legends.[8] Intended for older children, it is beautifully illustrated and intersperses factual stories of her father's childhood with Lakota tales.

While Rosebud remained in New York, her sisters made their lives elsewhere. After spending a year at City College, Chauncina married Lee White Horse, an Arapaho from Oklahoma, and, like Rosebud, found employment in show business. They traveled to rodeos and circuses performing an impalement act: as she stood steady against a wall, her husband outlined her body with arrows. Chauncina later commented, "That was back when I didn't have sense enough to be afraid," adding, "In the Depression a person learned to do a lot of things."

The White Horses eventually settled in Chicago, where Chauncina found a job she enjoyed selling advertising for Yellow Pages customers and laying out ads for publication. She became a vocal and effective spokesperson for the Chicago Indian community. She retired in 1974 and the next year began work at the Chicago Indian Health Service, where she served as assistant director.[9] In 1980, a year before her death, she addressed the Conference on Urban Indians held at the Center for the History of the American Indian at the Newberry Library, Chicago. Her talk underscored the needs of elderly urban Indians, those who had come to the cities to look for work during World War II or who had been part of the official Bureau of Indian Affairs relocation program, which began in 1952. These elders, she explained, "are transitional people, standing with one foot in the tribal ways and one foot in the dominant White world."[10] Her talk proved to be a call that was answered by the establishment at the Newberry Library of an American Indian Oral History Project.[11]

Evelyn's life took a very different path. Growing up in New York City, without the influence of her father, her Indian identity was less strong than that of her sisters. At Mount Holyoke College she majored in Speech Pathology and graduated magna cum laude in 1942. She continued her studies at Northwestern University, where she completed both an M.A. and a Ph.D., and taught at Mount Holyoke and Vassar. Still, in 1946 the Indian Council Fire in Chicago presented her with a Life Achievement Award, and the next year Vassar College awarded her a grant to travel to the Pine Ridge and Rosebud Reservations to record Dakota songs, history, and stories told by some of the oldest Indians there. Several of the songs were recorded during the annual sun dance.[12]

In 1954, Evelyn received a Fulbright Fellowship to study the physiology of the larynx in Paris; she also lectured at medical centers in England, Germany, Holland, and Italy. When she returned to the United States, she was appointed lecturer in otolaryngology and assistant director of the Voice Clinic, Northwestern University Medical School. There she met Dr. Hans Finkbeiner, a German obstetrician and gynecologist. They were married in New York and subsequently moved to Germany, where she and her husband opened a cytology laboratory in addition to his medical practice. She continues to live in Germany to this day.

The Jones Beach Indian Village made such an impact on the children of Long Island for two decades that its memory was preserved and cherished. In 1983 I decided to make it the subject of my master's thesis in anthropology.[13] When I mentioned the project to friends, the reply would often be, "You're writing about *my* Rosebud? How is she? Where is she?" Those who as children in the 1930s and 1940s had visited Jones Beach knew her, and each had a personal Rosebud story to tell. Todd Berks, wife of sculptor Robert Berks, told me, "We all believed without a doubt that Rosebud saw us as individuals and that she responded to us singularly. With all the children who came to the Indian Village each day, it was not likely that

Rosebud knew each one individually, but we each knew in our hearts that we were special to her."

In 1983 one of Sharon Monahan's "And That's the Way It Was" columns in the *New York Times* dealt with memories of Jones Beach: "When we were tired of the horseplay in the pool and our lips turned purple and our fingertips shriveled and turned a pallid pink, we headed for the Indian Village. The village spread out over the grass in front of the outdoor roller skating rink, next to the bandshell, near the Central Mall. The Princess, attired in a deerskin dress, moccasins, feathers and real black braids, taught us arts and crafts in genuine tepees."[14]

In a subsequent letter to the editor, Barbara Goldstein Paltrow wrote, "Those of us who grew up during the 30's and 40's in the then sparsely populated communities along the South Shore of Long Island shared a posh private summer camp, enormous in size, diverse in facilities, activities and entertainment, all at an absurdly low price, courtesy of the State of New York." She remembered Rosebud as a "true Cherokee princess": "This splendid woman, always attired in her authentic Indian garments, was full of grace and elegance and was wondrously articulate."[15] I, too, contributed a letter to the *Times* that year, noting that Rosebud was seventy-six years old "and still going strong."[16]

Rosebud herself wrote the last letter of the series:

It is indeed rewarding to find that after four or five decades, the beach and a person – who is very honored – are remembered in such a beautiful way.

The thousands of children who came to Jones Beach and the Indian Village in the 20 years I was there were a part of my family. The games, the storytelling, the hours of creating baskets, belts, and war bonnets in the arts and crafts classes were a way to introduce them to the old lore and life of the Native Americans. Barbara called it "Our Indian Village" – so it was.

As in the old Indian saying, "All nature was witness to our deeds and thoughts," the spirit of those wonderful days will always live in our hearts.

A correction please. I am Lakota-Sioux and I was and am always called Rosebud, never Princess. . . .

To my many young friends, who are now grown, I say: "My hands hold yours."[17]

Rosebud spoke frequently and earnestly about her wish to learn more about her parents and grandparents and to write a book about them. Through many years she had gathered information from relatives and friends of both families. Now she needed to travel to archives and governmental agencies to locate source material, and she enlisted me in the project. We began with resources in New York, including the library of the Museum of the American Indian, then located in The Bronx.

In the early 1980s, we went to Washington DC, where, among the Office of Indian Affairs records in the National Archives, Rosebud was thrilled to find the original Rosebud Reservation enrollment records and allotment maps. These documented each parcel of allotted land and its division among the descendants of the original owners, thereby enabling Rosebud to discern relationships based on the fractionated land shares.[18] This information became the basis for seeking out relatives in South Dakota.

In late April 1983, Rosebud and I made a trip to South Dakota. In Pierre, the capital, we examined records in the state archives relating to the Yellow Robe family. In Rapid City we went to see the building dedicated to her father's memory, the River Ridge High Rise for the Elderly, which contains fifty-six apartments and a kitchen where meals are prepared for the residents. It was built by the Pennington County Housing and Redevelopment Commission following the Rapid City flood of 1972, which destroyed a portion of the downtown area. On June 9, 1975, the mayor of Rapid City dedicated the building to Chauncey Yellow Robe's memory. Harold Shunk, a student many years earlier at the Rapid City Indian School, had submitted the name of his old friend and mentor for this honor. Etched in a bronze plaque prominently located in the building's lobby is the photograph of Chauncey with his father that was taken upon Chauncey's return from Carlisle. Rosebud was deeply moved by this honor given to her father and grandfather. No less were the feelings aroused by our visit to her parents' graves at the Mountain View Cemetery nearby.

Arrangements had been made for us to meet for dinner with the Yellow Robe family of Rapid City. We were a large group, and there were very few other people in the hotel dining room. Mary Yellow Robe introduced us to her sons and daughters and their families. After we ordered, there was excitement in the corridor: Luke Yellow Robe, a police officer at the time, told us that the hotel had just received a bomb threat. We retreated quickly to the parking lot, where we waited to find out what to do next. After several minutes we were told that a disgruntled employee had been apprehended for making the threat, and we were able to return to our dinner. As we waited for our food, I stood up and spoke to the assembled Yellow Robe family: "I have heard of several ways of being welcomed into the tribe, but never have I heard of being inducted by 'bomb threat.' You really did not have to go to all this trouble!"

For the next several days we visited the buildings that had originally been part of the Rapid City Indian Boarding School. It was where Rosebud had been born and where she lived throughout her childhood and adolescent years. We were even able to find the one-room schoolhouse where she had gone to elementary school, now remodeled into a restaurant. At breakfasts and lunches we visited with Rosebud's many friends who came to Rapid City to see us, including members of the Iron Plume family from the Pine Ridge Reservation. Shirley Plume and her daughter Emma (Pinkie) enjoyed spending time with Rosebud and took us on a tour of Rapid City, enlivened by many wonderful stories.

Rosebud had long wanted to return to the places she remembered from her college years, so next we flew to Sioux Falls, where we were met by Emogene Paulson, director of the Indian Institute at the University of South Dakota, who escorted us to Vermillion. Emogene's first contact with Rosebud had been in 1975, when she featured Rosebud in her column "Who's Who among the Sioux," published in the institute's quarterly newsletter.

Gen. Lloyd Moses, who had known Rosebud in their years as students together at the university, was director emeritus of the Indian Institute and had arranged for a luncheon in honor of Rosebud's return to Vermillion.[19] Happily, her visit coincided with the annual "Indian Awareness Week" sponsored by the Tiyospaye Council, the Native students' association. Rosebud was gratified to meet some of the current students, to listen to their concerns and offer them advice. Altogether, her visit to the University of South Dakota was both sentimental and fulfilling.

In May 1989 she was invited to return to Vermillion to be awarded the honorary degree of Doctor of Humane Letters. Her nomination for that honor recognized her work to preserve tradition and promote understanding between Indians and whites.[20] I accompanied her, and many of her friends from near and far attended, as did her granddaughter, Karen, and my son Bruce, who videotaped the ceremonies. Rosebud's sister Evelyn came from Germany to join the celebration. The 102d annual commencement exercises were held on campus May 13, in the Dakotadome. This was the centennial year for the graduate school, which had granted its first master's degree in 1889.

General Moses presented the doctoral hood and degree to Rosebud before an audience of nine hundred graduates, their families, and friends. He read a citation detailing Rosebud's life, which concluded, "The University of South Dakota pays tribute to this woman for the honor she has brought to this institution and to the Indian and non-Indian people whose lives she has touched." Moses escorted Rosebud from the platform, and although she used a cane, she walked with head high and appeared younger than her eighty-two years.

Rosebud Yellow Robe Day, a part of the graduation weekend, had been proclaimed in the local newspapers, on the printed invitations sent to special guests, on local cable television, and on printed handbills posted in university buildings and stores all over town. At a celebration held in the new building of the W. H. Over State Museum, there were speeches of welcome and praise, and Sioux songs and dances were performed by local Native individuals.[21] The museum director explained that the honorary degree had been presented to Rosebud "for a lifetime commitment in communicating the values of her people to non-Indians, and, as a consequence, she serves as a powerful model for Native Americans who seek ways to preserve their culture. It also honors the Lakota people who are fortunate in having produced such a person."

Professor Joseph Cash, acting director of the Institute of Indian Studies, and General Moses both spoke in honor of Rosebud. Then Moses escorted her to the podium. Dressed in a black sheath with a brilliant red jacket, she appeared radiant as she approached the microphone. She spoke in a firm, strong voice:

With a glad heart I greet you. I wish that my father were here. He was born in 1867 in a skin tipi in what is now the state of Montana. He lived the life of an Indian boy until he went to Carlisle to study. He stayed with his people for most of his life in an educational environment.

I came to the University of South Dakota in 1925. Then there were only two of us [Indians].

Education was very important to my father. He always said to listen to the stories of all peoples. Accept the best they have to offer. After all, we are one family. We are all relatives. . . . Since 1925, there has been much more understanding of our ways. It is wonderful to see this museum. Here our crafts are being continued. I knew Dr. Over. Both my father and I knew him. We also knew the Clarks whose collection is here.[22] Indian art flowed from the Indians' being into their work. I accept this great honor for the Lakota people, particularly for the Lakota women. They were the real power in tribal life. The men were important, but they were supported by the work of the women.

She concluded, "With all things and all beings we shall be as relatives. I greet the highest in you."

During those days in Vermillion in May 1989, everything focused on Rosebud. Her achievements, her family, her friends, her life were portrayed as though pictured on a theater screen. Everywhere she went, she passed her picture on bulletin boards, in the museum, and in the store windows. For this brief time, Rosebud was the most celebrated individual in town.[23]

Believing that birthdays were meant to celebrate, I always made sure that some of Rosebud's friends got together for a luncheon on her birthday, February 26.[24] On the occasion of her seventieth, I chartered a minibus to take the members of "the Birthday Club" to the American Museum of Natural History for lunch in the museum's restaurant. After we had eaten and the birthday cake ceremony was over, we begged Rosebud to tell us some of her stories, and she regaled us with new tales and old.

One year we held the birthday party at a restaurant called "Rosebud" in the Westbury Hotel in Manhattan. Coincidentally, it was the hotel in which Rosebud had first stayed when she came to New York. Many of the other parties were given in my home with a different theme each year. One of the most memorable was Rosebud's eightieth, when my son Robert created a "Rosebud sled" cake, complete with runners and a cord to pull it, all made out of frosting.

Not long before Rosebud's eighty-third birthday I was discussing my Jones Beach Indian Village research with a group of friends when one of them, a highly respected local surgeon, said, "My Rosebud! You know my Rosebud? Tell me, how is she, where is she?" Soon thereafter, he came face to face with "his" Rosebud at her party, and you could see the child in him returning as he embraced her. Boyhood memories of Jones Beach and days spent at the Indian Village came pouring out in waves.

As we gathered for Rosebud's eighty-fifth birthday, we all seemed to realize that this was one we would especially remember. It turned out to be her last. Bette Midler's "You Are the Wind beneath My Wings" played throughout the afternoon, telling Rosebud that for us she was indeed the wind beneath our wings! We sat for many hours trying to hold on to those precious moments.[25]

Rosebud's final professional appearance was at New York University's Graduate Film Forum. In the early spring of 1992 she was invited to introduce a showing of the restored version of *The Silent Enemy*.[26] She agreed enthusiastically, even though she had begun to experience the symptoms of her final illness. When we arrived at the theater, it was overflowing with an eager audience that included both anthropology graduate students and film students from the Tisch School of the Arts at NYU. Rosebud, beautiful in a simple black dress and black fur hat, requested a chair, her only accommodation to her physical problems.

As she introduced the film, the theater fell quiet. She spoke clearly, in a strong voice and with much emotion, sensing the excitement of this audience. The students brought to *The Silent Enemy* a background and interest that other groups had lacked. Rosebud spoke about her father and how he came to be in the film and how difficult working in the frigid weather and harsh conditions of Lake Temagami had been for him and the rest of the cast and crew. The audience was mesmerized as she continued with stories of her father's life.

The students asked questions with respect and knowledge. Rosebud was delighted with their response to her introduction, and she became even more animated. Perhaps she realized that she would not likely speak in front of an audience again, for she gave it all she had. After the film was shown and Rosebud had answered some final questions, it was obvious that she was exhausted. As we whisked her away to return home, Rosebud said, "That was one of the most responsive audiences I've ever spoken to."

It was her last and best performance.

Only days after the talk at NYU, Rosebud began to feel more and more uncomfortable; she never regained her usual pep. Her doctor diagnosed the flu, but after several weeks during which she felt worse, a consultation with another doctor ended in exploratory surgery, performed on April 6, 1992. When she awoke from the anesthesia in the intensive care unit, the first thing she said to me was, "Do you know what day this is?" I said, "Yes, April 6th." Rosebud, in one look, told me she was afraid that she was going to die on that date, just as both her parents had, three years apart and many years ago. I continued talking and said, "Rosebud, you know it's my birthday. Aren't you going to say, 'Happy Birthday'?" We laughed, and for a moment the dark idea that she might die that day passed. A short time later we learned from the surgeon that Rosebud had pancreatic cancer and probably would live no more than six months.

We were stunned, but Rosebud, realizing that she had a terminal illness, was realistic and began to plan for her remaining days. Her sister Evelyn had come from Germany and arranged for Rosebud to spend some time in a local nursing home, where family and friends could visit. After a brief stay there, however, Rosebud needed intensive care, and Evelyn arranged for her to enter hospice care at Calvary Hospital in The Bronx.

The weeks before Rosebud entered Calvary were difficult ones. No patient left there alive; one could be admitted only if a doctor specified that the patient had only six or fewer months to live. Rosebud was brave but frightened. One afternoon before the move to Calvary she and I were talking quietly. I said, "Rosebud, remember all the adventures we've had together, our trips to South Dakota, to the National Archives in Washington DC for your family research, and to all your lecture sites? I promise you I will be with you through this adventure too!"

The time Rosebud spent at Calvary, six months almost to the day, was more like an adventure than we expected. At least in the beginning, it was like visiting an unreal resort. There were scheduled events, such as "Bingo Days," and the menu was unlimited in variety. Each day that summer we spent several hours in the open garden, hearing lectures, playing bingo, doing crafts, or just talking. Almost every day for six months we visited, and when Rosebud could no longer converse, I simply sat there with her. I was comforted just by being in her presence and believe that she too found comfort in our silent companionship.

We were very fortunate, Rosebud and I, to find Canon Ed, an Episcopal cleric from Ireland who had come to learn how to help the dying and their families. He established an immediate rapport with Rosebud and me and became our spiritual mentor and dear friend. For the six weeks he was at Calvary he listened to and supported us. He would talk with Rosebud alone for an hour or so and then spend some time listening to me. Often he comforted me when I thought there could be no comfort. We both came to lean on him for advice and solace. He seemed to impart his strength of spirit to us.[27]

Rosebud was deeply religious. The week before her death she asked me to get her the Indian version of the Twenty-third Psalm. I called the American Indian Community House for a copy and gave it to her.[28] I know she was comforted by it.

Although I visited her daily, I had a constant dread that Rosebud would die alone, so near the end I spent every night from midnight to five or six in the morning at the hospital. When Rosebud died in the early hours of October 5, 1992, her daughter Buddy, granddaughter Karen, and I were with her. Our final adventure together was over.

A service of memorial and thanksgiving for Rosebud's life was held on October 29, 1992, at St. Luke's Church in Forest Hills Gardens, New York. I presented this tribute:

Remembering Rosebud is something I will do each day for the rest of my life. . . . She spent her life communicating the true picture of Native American culture to people of other cultures. In doing so, she became a role model for other young Indians. Her pride, knowledge, and forward-looking approach to contemporary Indian life inspired others to emulate her. She wanted people to know that Indians were alive and well in the modern professions, not just relics of the past. . . .

Finally, let me share with you these words written by Ralph Waldo Emerson: "To laugh often and love much; to win the respect of persons and the affection of children; . . . to know that even one life has breathed easier because you have lived – this is to have succeeded."

Afterward, I made the trip to South Dakota for the final tribute and burial of Rosebud's ashes near her parents. At the memorial service in the Lakota Episcopal Church in Rapid City, Deborah Yellow Robe sang "Wind beneath My Wings." She did not know it was the song we had played for Rosebud on her eighty-fifth birthday.

I sought solace in Santa Fe, New Mexico, a place that Rosebud also loved. She knew I had built a home there and that a magnificent portrait of her as she looked in her later years hung prominently in the living room. It was painted by Ann McCoy, a renowned artist who met Rosebud while searching for an American Indian model; they had become good friends during Rosebud's final years. Rosebud had told me in one of our many emotional conversations that she would always be with me in Santa Fe because her picture was there.[29]

When she died, forty-five years after our first meeting that summer in 1947, she had become my dearest friend, my second mother, and the person I tried the most to emulate. Many others have looked up to Rosebud as a role model for their own lives. To this day, when I talk about Rosebud – and I do, no matter where I am – her influence is evident in the many people "of a certain age" who knew her at Jones Beach, heard her lectures in schools or museums, and never forgot her.

Epilogue
Keeping the Promise

From the very first time that Rosebud mentioned her research files and her wish to fill in the history of her family, I was absorbed in the project with her. I still am. Even after her death, as I continued the work that she herself had begun so many years before, new leads constantly came to light, as though she were guiding me along. Here, in sequence, are some of the places and events to which I was led.

RETURN TO SOUTH DAKOTA

In May 1993 I attended the graduation exercises at Sinte Gleska University, located on the Rosebud Reservation in South Dakota.[1] It was my first visit to the place for which Rosebud had been named and offered a good opportunity to spend time with the Yellow Robe family and continue my research.

I flew to Rapid City, where the Yellow Robes met me, and we started out for the Rosebud Reservation. Deborah (Deb), her mother Mary, and sister Cookie were enthusiastic about the trip. The weather was perfect, and after several hours I noticed two eagles off to the side of the road, seemingly leading our car. Deb commented, "That is a very good sign."

The graduation activities were unique in their combination of academic and Lakota traditions. After a traditional feast we made our way to a rodeo and powwow. Deb initiated the ceremonies by singing "The Star Spangled Banner." I was introduced to several of the participants in the rodeo, and it was great fun to follow their progress in the competitions.

This first of many powwows I have now attended was electrifying. I had not been prepared for the serious religious dimension of the occasion. The energy released by the dancers in their colorful dress was contagious to the entire audience. I felt comfortable and welcome, although a trifle self-conscious as one of the very few non-Indian visitors.

The next morning we attended Sunday services at the Episcopal Church and were invited to the home of the pastor and his wife for brunch. On the way back to Rapid City, Deb offered to drive me by way of Pierre for another visit to the archives. This trip to South Dakota became another memorable part of the ongoing treasure hunt.[2]

ROSEBUD'S SONG

One day Ann McCoy, the painter, called me in Santa Fe to ask if her friend, Jacques d'Amboise, founder of the National Dance Institute, might come to my home to see her portrait of Rosebud. I did not know then that she had spoken to Jacques about using Rosebud's life as a theme for his 1994 international children's dance event.

Jacques came to see the portrait, and after several hours spent talking about Rosebud and looking at other pictures of her, he invited us to visit a school in Santa Fe where he was rehearsing a dance program. We spent the next morning watching how wonderfully the children responded to their dance instructors, and how pleased they seemed to be with the chance to perform for an audience.

When Jacques asked me to help with a National Dance Institute production to be called *Rosebud's Song*, I agreed enthusiastically and wrote a biographical sketch of Rosebud for the program. Some one thousand schoolchildren participated in the performance, many from the New York area but others from countries around the world, including Nepal, Siberia, Chile, and Ethiopia. Taking inspiration from Native traditions that express the unity of humankind with the natural world, the pageant sought "to represent through dance the earth and its peoples in all its discordant harmony."[3] Choreographers had worked with children in their home countries to prepare them, and the international students came to New York a month in advance for rehearsals and to meet local students and participate in events at local schools.[4] The students themselves created the scenic backdrop for the program: a muslin screen as long as a city block, made up of two-foot squares, each a self-portrait.

On May 22, 1994, Madison Square Garden was filled to capacity. Rosebud's family and friends had come from South Dakota, and her many friends from the New York area were also assembled for the event.[5] The performance exceeded all our expectations and was a fitting memorial to a woman whose life had been dedicated to teaching children.

FINDING LILLIE SPRINGER'S LETTERS

Shortly after the performance of "Rosebud's Song," Clara Turner, the daughter of Lillie Springer's childhood friend Clara Henneman, contacted me. She had seen the publicity in *Parade*, the nationwide Sunday newspaper supplement, and decided to find someone who had known Rosebud.

Her mother, who died in 1971, had corresponded with Lillie Springer from 1905 to 1927 and kept her letters. Now they were sent to me. It was amazing to learn in Lillie's own words how she felt about the extraordinary events in her life. One letter included several pieces of fabric, samples from her wedding dress. There were also two letters written by Chauncey after Lillie's death. It seems a true miracle that these letters found their way to me.

A PROMINENT SOUTH DAKOTA FAMILY

The 1996 theme for the annual conference held at the Center for Western Studies, Augustana College, Sioux Falls, South Dakota, was "Prominent South Dakota Families." I read the title aloud to myself, recognizing a perfect opportunity to share the results of my study of the Yellow Robe family. The organizers invited me to deliver a talk at the conference luncheon.

The Rapid City Yellow Robes offered to meet my husband and me in Sioux Falls, and we spent several days together. To my delight they attended my talk about their family. My son Bruce flew in from college to videotape the event.

The audience of South Dakotans interested in their state's history were enthusiastic, but most had never heard of the Yellow Robes. Rosebud had left her home state after the Coolidge ceremony in 1927 and had returned only a few times. That she had been born in Rapid City, had never lived on a reservation, was educated in the Rapid City public schools, and then attended the University of South Dakota – only a little more than an hour's drive from Sioux Falls – came as a surprise to many in attendance.

Earlier in the day a portrait of an Indian woman that had been in the school's collection since the 1920s was brought out of storage for me to examine. Although the painting is not a good likeness, the skin dress resembles the one that Rosebud had worn for the Coolidge ceremony in 1927.

That the portrait seemed, indeed, to represent Rosebud solved the mystery of its identity. Now, I thought, Rosebud's circle had been made complete. The Yellow Robes had been restored to their rightful place among the prominent families of South Dakota.

CONTINUING THE TREASURE HUNT AT YALE UNIVERSITY

One afternoon in 1997 Betty Clark Rosenthal, daughter of the missionary Clarks, called me excitedly from her home in Santa Fe, New Mexico. Rosebud's parents and Betty's had been friends from the time they all lived in South Dakota during the early 1900s. The two families had kept in touch throughout the years, visiting in New York each summer. During my trips to Santa Fe I became good friends with Betty, who many years before had earned a doctorate in anthropology at Harvard University. She knew about my research and had just learned that Richard Pratt's papers had been given to the Beinecke Library at Yale. Here was another clue to pursue on the treasure hunt.

Not long thereafter I headed for New Haven with Joan Lehn, a fellow anthropologist. My cousin Beverly Weinberg met us at the New Haven railroad station, drove us to the library, and offered her help. We found that the large Pratt Collection did include voluminous correspondence with Chauncey. How exciting it was to read those handwritten letters that document the long and close relationship between the two men and the respect they had for each other. Chauncey's letters express devotion to his "school Father"; Pratt was Chauncey's mentor, just as Rosebud had been mine.

THE YELLOW ROBE SUMMIT AT SANTA FE

In spring 1998 I invited some of the women of the Yellow Robe family to spend a weekend together at my home in Santa Fe. I hoped that new material might come to light as they shared family stories in relaxed circumstances. Fawn White Horse Sitman, a daughter of Chauncina, came from Phoenix, Arizona. Shirley Plume, the wife of Rosebud's cousin Paul Plume, came from the Pine Ridge Reservation, and her daughter Paulette Plume, who lived in Santa Fe part time, also accepted the invitation. Joan Lehn came from New York as well.

The welcoming dinner at a local restaurant proved a congenial venue for sharing stories. We found that sitting around a table induced our best recollections. We even included Evelyn several times during our discussions, speaking with her at length by telephone at her home in Germany.

We spent the next day and a half reminiscing about legends and stories already familiar to me. In the end I realized that Rosebud had been very thorough in telling me the family stories.

"THE WIND BENEATH MY WINGS"

For many years I believed that the memory of the Indian Village at Jones Beach was alive and well. In 1997, on the anniversary of Rosebud's death, I visited the beach with my friend Janet Marks and went to the area where the Indian Village had been. There was no trace of the tipis, the story area, the craft workshops, or the turtle races. At the Castles in the Sand Museum, located in the old East Bathhouse, Rosebud was remembered with only a small photo and a short segment of a video. It made me very sad, and I was determined not to let her memory be lost. I set up a conference with the park director, Frank Kollar, and made my case for recognizing Rosebud's important part in the history of Jones Beach and the influence she had had on so many Long Island youngsters. When Kollar asked me what was so special about Rosebud, I replied, "She taught people to be proud of their own heritage. She had the ability to engage young and old almost immediately. It was her 'star' quality." In the end, he was receptive to my suggestion.

On August 28, 1998, at the Castles in the Sand Museum, Bernadette Castro, commissioner of the New York State Office of Parks, Recreation, and Historic Preservation, accepted a plaque honoring Rosebud. Her daughter and granddaughter proudly attended the presentation. The plaque reads: "In appreciation of Rosebud Yellow Robe, director 1930–1950 of the Jones Beach Indian Village, with love and admiration of the thousands who learned from her teachings."[6]

A festive luncheon followed, served on the beach under a tent to protect guests from the sun and the wind, which unexpectedly became so strong that four beach employees literally had to hold down the corner poles to keep the canopy from blowing away. We could only look at one another with the same thought: she must be here – still the wind beneath our wings.

THE TRAIN TRIP TO CARLISLE

On Tuesday, September 14, 1999, Evelyn Robe Finkbeiner and I met in Manhattan's Penn Station and boarded a train to begin our journey to Carlisle, Pennsylvania. Changing trains in Philadelphia, we continued on to Harrisburg, where Barbara Landis, Carlisle Indian School research specialist for the Cumberland County Historical Society, met us. She was our guide as we reconstructed Chauncey's school days at Carlisle. Although his trip from the Rosebud Reservation over a century ago was much longer than ours, our train ride made us think of his first railroad journey.

I had gone to Carlisle eighteen years earlier to do research, but since that time new material had become available. More important, through e-mail and phone conversations, Barbara and I had established a friendship, and it was she who helped us arrange this trip back in time.

We drove to Carlisle from Harrisburg and spent most of the day touring the grounds of the present War College, whose buildings once housed the Carlisle Indian School and where, Barbara told us, much has remained the same. We next drove to the Cumberland Historical Building, where books and other materials were waiting for us, all documenting Chauncey's accomplishments both at school and after his graduation.

Coincidentally, that afternoon a bus carrying a large group of Menominee Indians came to hear and see a slide lecture about school days at Carlisle. Several whose grandparents had been enrolled at the school were making this trip to honor their memory. During the slide presentation, Chauncey's picture was shown in various activities on the campus and throughout the years. Evelyn was introduced to the audience as his youngest daughter, and she was visibly touched by their warm and enthusiastic interest in her father.

We spent the rest of our time following up on more research leads, walking around town, and getting a feel for what it might have been like for Chauncey in the 1880s and 1890s.

The never-ending treasure hunt has only paused here. Even as I write this conclusion to the chronicle of Rosebud Yellow Robe and her family, I feel certain that pertinent information will continue to surface. But now is the time to share this story, a truly American saga.

I have kept the promise I made to Rosebud.

Notes

PREFACE

1. David Thomson, *Rosebud: The Story of Orson Welles* (New York: Alfred A. Knopf, 1996), p. 150.

2. Edward Castle, "Rosebud: Solution to Mystery Offered; Tattered CBS Radio Ledger Tells Tale of 'Rosebud' Roots," *Las Vegas Sun*, August 11, 1991, p. 1A.

INTRODUCTION

1. In 1935, John Search the Enemy, aged ninety-eight, a Lakota from the Rosebud Reservation, signed a typed, notarized deposition declaring that Chauncey Yellow Robe's mother, whose name is here given as Slow Bear, "was a full sister of the father of Sitting Bull, the famous Sioux Indian Chieftain" (There is also a manuscript in the handwriting of Chauncey Yellow Robe, Rosebud Yellow Robe Family Papers, privately held; copy in the author's possession).

2. "Ella Deloria," in Marion E. Gridley, ed. and comp., *Indians of Today* (Chicago: Millar, 1947), p. 30; Ella C. Deloria, *Speaking of Indians* (New York: Friendship Press, 1944).

3. "Te Ata (Mary Thompson)," in Gridley, *Indians of Today*, p. 83.

4. "Ruth Muskrat Bronson," in Gridley, *Indians of Today*, p. 14; Ruth Muskrat Bronson, *Indians Are People, Too* (New York: Friendship Press, 1947).

5. Office of Indian Affairs to Marjorie Frogel [Weinberg], September 11, 1947. The Chauncey Yellow Robe obituary originally appeared in the *Martin (South Dakota) Messenger* and was reprinted in the *Indian Leader*, May 2, 1930.

6. Rosebud had been given the privilege of wearing a warbonnet on the occasion of the 1927 ceremony inducting President Calvin Coolidge into the Lakota tribe (see chaper 3).

7. Marjorie Weinberg, "Rosebud Yellow Robe and the Jones Beach Indian Village"(master's thesis, New York University, 1990).

8. Rosebud Yellow Robe, preface to Elaine Mei Aoki et al., *Write Idea!* (New York: Macmillan/McGraw-Hill School Publishing, 1993), pp. i–iii.

1. WHITE THUNDER TO YELLOW ROBE

1. George E. Hyde, *Spotted Tail's Folk: A History of the Brulé Sioux* (Norman: University of Oklahoma Press, 1961), p. 5.

2. J. H. Bratley, a schoolteacher on the Rosebud Reservation, came into possession of Swift Bear's winter count and showed it to Yellow Robe, among others, for an interpretation of the pictographs. A copy was published by Lucy Cohen, "Swift Bear Winter Count," *Indians at Work*, January 1942, p. 14, and February 1942, p. 30. Marcella Cash, archivist at Sinte Gleska University, Rosebud, South Dakota, notes that even though Swift Bear was from a different band, the Yellow Robes were able to use Swift Bear's winter count to validate and date important events in their own family's history.

3. Ruth Brown, biography manuscript of Chauncey Yellow Robe, 1929, Rosebud Yellow Robe Family Papers.

4. According to the Lakota kinship system, Rosebud considered Luke Yellow Robe a grandson. In the majority culture he would be a cousin.

5. Yellow Robe remains a Lakota name to this day, although there are more Yellow Robes among the Crows in Montana than among the Lakotas in South Dakota.

6. John S. Gray, *Centennial Campaign: The Sioux War of 1876* (Norman: University of Oklahoma Press, 1988), p. 196. The Rosebud mentioned here is Rosebud Creek, a tributary of the White River, not the Rosebud River in Montana. The Crazy Horse fight refers to the attack by Col. J. J. Reynolds on a camp presumed to be that of Crazy Horse, March 17, the first military engagement of the campaign of 1876.

7. James C. Olson, *Red Cloud and the Sioux Problem* (Lincoln: University of Nebraska Press, 1965), gives a good account of the 1876 military campaign against the Lakotas.

8. James R. Walker, *Lakota Belief and Ritual*, ed. Raymond J. DeMallie and Elaine A. Jahner (Lincoln: University of Nebraska Press, 1980), pp. 6–13.

9. Richard H. Pratt, *The Indian Industrial School, Carlisle, Pennsylvania*, intro. Robert M. Utley (1908; reprint, Carlisle PA: Cumberland County Historical Society, 1979).

10. Pratt, *Indian Industrial School*, pp. 16–17, 20.

11. Luther Standing Bear, *My People the Sioux* (Boston: Houghton Mifflin, 1928), presents a detailed account of life at the Carlisle Indian School and of recruiting visits to the Rosebud Reservation.

12. The date of Yellow Robe's death, according to census records, was provided by Marcella Cash, archivist, Sinte Gleska University letter to author, December 13, 2002.

2. CHAUNCEY YELLOW ROBE

1. Chauncey Yellow Robe, "My Boyhood Days," *Indian Leader*, October 30, 1925, reprinted as "Grand-Nephew of 'Sitting Bull' Is a Leading Educator," *American Indian*, December 1926, 5, 12. The following quotations, including his story of the buffalo kill, are taken from this source.

2. According to census records, Yellow Robe's first wife, *Thašína* (Her Robe), bore him three children but died young. He then married Chauncey's mother (called Slow Bear in the census report but always referred to by Chauncey as Tachawin), who bore him seven children, and her sister Grabbing Bear, who bore him eight children (Cash letter, December 13, 2002).

3. Clearly a reference to the *huká* ceremony, a formal adoption that honored a child and made him part of a special privileged class (Walker, *Lakota Belief and Ritual*, pp. 216–41).

4. Chauncey's sled was given to the Museum of the American Indian, in New York City.

5. Brown, manuscript biography of Chauncey Yellow Robe.

6. Chauncey Yellow Robe, "My Boyhood Days," p. 14.

7. Richard Yellow Robe (Search the Enemy), "An Indian Boy's Experience," *Indian Helper* 3, no. 17 (1887).

8. Brown, manuscript biography of Chauncey Yellow Robe.

9. Chauncey Yellow Robe, "My Boyhood Days," p. 14.

10. Brown, manuscript biography of Chauncey Yellow Robe.

11. Fergus M. Bordewich, *Killing the White Man's Indian: Reinventing Native Americans at the End of the Twentieth Century* (New York: Doubleday, 1996), p. 284.

12. Bordewich, *Killing the White Man's Indian*, p. 284.

13. Jewel H. Grutman, *The Ledgerbook of Thomas Blue Eagle* (Atlanta GA: Lickle, 1994), is a modern creation inspired by ledger drawings in the Richard H. Pratt Manuscript Collection, Beinecke Library, Yale University, New Haven CT, and by material held by the Cumberland County Historical Society, Carlisle PA.

14. Chauncey Yellow Robe to Richard H. Pratt, 1910. All correspondence cited between Yellow Robe and Pratt is in the Pratt Collection.

15. Evidence of their mutual admiration, loyalty, and respect is revealed in letters written years later. Pratt wrote to Yellow Robe in January 1919: "When I remember back to your arrival at Carlisle, and the conditions from which you came and realize your transformation, entirely due to your venture into a long absence from home and placing yourself under a radically different environment from anything possible on your reservation, and see the wonderful success of it all, it establishes to me, at least, beyond a peradventure, that all the Indians have ever needed has been just that sort of education."

16. Brown, manuscript biography of Yellow Robe.

17. *Indian Helper* 6, no. 12 (1890).

18. The boarding school experience worked for Chauncey, as it did for many others, including Luther Standing Bear, a fellow Lakota, and Olympic champion Jim Thorpe. See Standing Bear, *My People the Sioux*; and Robert W. Wheeler, *Jim Thorpe: World's Greatest Athlete* (Norman: University of Oklahoma Press, 1988). As the first generation of educated Indians, they became successful and productive citizens who could navigate in both the white and Native American worlds, and role models for those who followed after them. Today, however, more than a century later, the legacy of boarding schools like Carlisle is in general one of bitterness because of their attempt to eradicate native languages and cultures. Most American Indians condemn the United States for inflicting a social experiment of forced acculturation on generations of their ancestors.

19. Chauncey's brother Richard left Carlisle to enlist in the Sixteenth Infantry, U.S. Army (*Indian Helper* 7, no. 20 [1892]). He died in 1893.

20. Rosebud Yellow Robe, *An Album of the American Indian* (New York: Franklin Watts, 1969), p. 65.

21. *Indian Helper* 13, no. 3 (1897).

22. *Indian Helper* 13, no. 45 (1898). A patron wrote enthusiastically to Pratt: "Mr. Yellowrobe, your inspector, called a short time ago, and I found him most entertaining. You certainly did more to show your patrons and American citizens generally the possibilities in the Indian, by sending him out, than you could possibly have done in any other way. Always before, I had believed that the saying about the Indian returning to his blanket was quite true, but now I know, that instead, he can become an educated gentleman without even the suggestion of 'blanket'! " (*Indian Helper* 13, no. 17 [1898]).

23. *Indian Helper* 13, no. 45 (1898).

24. Yellow Robe to Pratt, May 12, 1899; *Indian Helper* 14, no. 28 (1899).

25. Quoted in *Indian Helper* 15, no. 36 (1900).

26. The school had opened in 1898. See Scott Riney, *The Rapid City Indian School, 1898–1933* (Norman: University of Oklahoma Press, 1999).

27. *Rapid City Daily Journal*, February 5, 1924, p. 1

28. Brown, manuscript biography of Chauncey Yellow Robe.

3. LIFE IN SOUTH DAKOTA

1. Lillie apparently changed the spelling of her surname; her parents continued to use "Sprenger." See Hulda and Meta Sprenger, *On the Trail of the Sprengers* (Winterthur, Switzerland: Privately published, 2000).

2. Lillian Springer to Clara Hennemen, July 1905. Copies of their correspondence are in the possession of the author, thanks to Clara's daughter.

3. Harold Shunk, who was a student at the school at the time, told me that because he had caught Chauncey and Lillie "spooning," he was given special privileges, such as picking up the school mail in Rapid City.

4. *A History of Pennington County, South Dakota*, n.p., n.d. (c. 1985).

5. Manuscript in Rosebud Yellow Robe Family Papers.

6. Years later Chauncey told the story to Rosebud.

7. Chauncey Yellow Robe to Pratt, February 26, 1907; Lillian Springer Yellow Robe to Clara Henneman (Mrs. John Hoffman), 1907.

8. Chauncey Yellow Robe to Pratt, May 30, 1918.

9. Bessie Cornelius is a sister of Shirley Plume, whose husband, Paul Plume, a grandson of Iron Plume, was Rosebud's cousin.

10. Bessie Cornelius, interview with author, Rapid City SD, 1994.

11. *History of Pennington County*. Rosebud probably used these stories in writing *Tonweya and the Eagles* (New York: Dial Books for Young Readers, 1979).

12. Chauncey Yellow Robe to Pratt, November 30, 1920.

13. Chauncey Yellow Robe, "My Boyhood Days," p. 15.

14. Mildred Fielder, *Sioux Indian Leaders* (Seattle WA: Superior, 1975), pp. 114–16, 118. Fielder reproduces quotations used in an article by Bob Lee, "Sioux Spokesman Flays Cody and Miles over Indian War Film," *Rapid City Journal*, July 6, 1969; Lee was apparently quoting from a contemporary article published in an Albany newspaper.

15. "The Indian Messiah" was actually the Paiute prophet Wovoka, who initiated the Ghost Dance; the religion spread rapidly among the Plains Indians.

16. "Report of the Executive Committee," in Society of American Indians, *Proceedings of the Fourth Annual Conference of the Society of American Indians* (Madison WI: Society of American Indians, 1914).

17. Quoted in Bunny McBride, *Molly Spotted Elk: A Penobscot in Paris* (Norman: University of Oklahoma Press, 1995), p. 68.

18. Chauncey Yellow Robe to Pratt, January 19, 1917.

19. Mildred Fielder, "War Whoop," *Rapid City Journal*, May 11, 1969.

20. Fielder, *Sioux Indian Leaders*, p. 125.

21. Chauncey Yellow Robe to Pratt, March 19, 1923.

22. The Sioux were designated both Dakota and Lakota.

23. Ed Morrow, interview with author, 1988.

24. Rosebud learned the hoop dance from Godfrey Broken Rope, a student at the Rapid City Indian School; she learned the others by observing Indian dancers in Rapid City.

25. Chauncey Yellow Robe, letters to Clara Henneman postmarked September 20 and September 27, 1927.

26. The bonnet itself was made from thirty eagle tail feathers by Robert F. Backus of Florence, Colorado; two trails, each composed of thirty more eagle tail feathers, were added by Pretty Bull and White Thunder. Jack R. Williams, "The Greatest Bonnet Maker of Them All!" *American Indian Hobbyist* 4, nos. 7–8 (1958): 64–65.

27. Brown, manuscript biography of Chauncey Yellow Robe.

28. C. C. O'Harra, "President Coolidge in the Black Hills," *Black Hills Engineer*, November 1927.

4. NEW YORK

1. Rosebud continued to use her maiden name for professional purposes. Show business custom before the Second World War required women to appear to be unmarried.

2. It was the Iron Plume family with whom Chauncey was living when he killed his first buffalo.

3. McBride, *Molly Spotted Elk*.

4. Thomas G. Lamb, *Eight Bears: A Biography of E. W. Deming, 1860–1942* (Oklahoma City OK: Griffith Books, 1978), 90–91.

5. In 1965 I went to meet the Demings' daughter, Alden, who had stayed in touch with Rosebud throughout the years by holiday correspondence. Although I expected a demure and elderly woman, I found Alden Deming in the lobby of her apartment building, dressed in a bright red pant suit and smoking a cigarette in a long holder. She remembered the Yellow Robes as a gracious and charming family; guests frequently gathered around them out of curiosity and interest in their stories. She also remarked that the young men clamored for the attention of Yellow Robe's attractive daughters.

6. Quoted in Brown, manuscript biography of Chauncey Yellow Robe.

7. Chauncey Yellow Robe, letter to *Hot Springs (South Dakota) Star*, August 24, 1928.

8. Jonathan Richards, "Silence Is Golden," *New Mexican*, August 1996.

9. Long Lance (who also attended Carlisle), a well-publicized personage in both Canada and the United States, had made a name in the Canadian armed forces. He promoted himself as a Blackfoot Indian, which he was not. Although his lineage was in dispute, today he would probably be considered Lumbee. See Donald B. Smith, *Chief Buffalo Child Long Lance: The Glorious Impostor* (Red Deer AB, Canada: Red Deer Press, 1999).

10. Smith, *Chief Buffalo Child Long Lance*, pp. 244–45.

11. President Coolidge sent this tribute to the Yellow Robe family. Rosebud obtained a copy of the typescript and published it in *Tonweya and the Eagles*.

5. JONES BEACH

1. Rosebud admitted to me that she never thought about the political agenda behind the lectures. She needed the money, and that was sufficient motivation.

2. J. Leverett Nelson, *Nassau Daily Review*, August 12, 1930.

3. *Brooklyn Times*, September 4, 1932.

4. The documentary video *Jones Beach: An American Riviera* (POZ Productions, Inc., 1998), narrated by Eli Wallach, includes footage of Rosebud.

5. Annabel Parker McCann, *New York Times*, March 23, 1933.

6. Mabel Powers (Yehsennohwehs) published two volumes of stories, *Around an Iroquois Camp Fire* (New York: Frederick A. Stokes, 1923), and *Stories the Iroquois Tell Their Children* (New York: American Book Company, 1917).

7. I have retold this story from my memory.

8. McCann, *New York Times*, March 23, 1933.

9. "Indian Village–Jones Beach State Park," mimeographed flyer, 1947 season. Copy in the author's possession.

10. This is the story as Shirley Plume heard Rosebud tell it on the radio.

11. *Life* 4 (June 27, 1938): 21; *Time* 31 (June 27, 1938): 30.

6. LATER YEARS

1. Chester Whitehorn, "Her Name Is Rosebud," *Cue* (Long Island Edition), May 5, 1951.

2. The film was based on a popular novel by Elliott Arnold, *Blood Brother* (New York: Duell, Sloan & Pearce, 1947).

3. Quoted in an unidentified newspaper clipping, 1951, author's collection. That

year my father took our family on a car trip around the United States. We followed Rosebud in several cities where I found newspaper articles relating to her appearances. Unfortunately, I neglected to note full citations for the articles.

4. Undated newspaper clipping, *Globe-Democrat* (1951), author's collection.

5. Unidentified newspaper clipping, Milwaukee WI 1951, author's collection.

6. Coordinating Committee on American Indian Affairs, "Minutes of Meeting. Coordinating Committee on American Indian Affairs, October 20, 1948." typescript, Mary Cabot Wheelwright Collection, Wheelwright Museum of the American Indian, Santa Fe NM. I am grateful to Leatrice A. Armstrong, educational coordinator at the Wheelwright Museum, for drawing this document to my attention.

7. Quoted in Whitehorn, "Her Name Is Rosebud."

8. Rosebud Yellow Robe, *Tonweya and the Eagles,* has been translated into several languages and was selected as an American Library Association Notable Book in 1979.

9. Vance GoodIron, Assistant Director, Chicago Indian Health Service, March 14, 1975, announcement regarding Chauncina White Horse's appointment as the next assistant director. Copy in the author's possession.

10. Chauncina White Horse, "The Indians of Chicago: A Perspective," in *Urban Indians: Proceedings of the Third Annual Conference on Problems and Issues concerning American Indians Today,* Occasional Papers Series 4 (Chicago: Newberry Library Center for the History of the American Indian, 1981), pp. 78–81.

11. David R. Miller, associate director of the center, characterized Chauncina as the "force behind the project." Letter to author, August 8, 1983.

12. University of South Dakota, *Who's Who among the Sioux* (Pierre SD: State Publishing Co., 1988), s.v. Evelyn Yellow Robe Finkbeiner. The recordings were made in July and August 1947 on thirty-three acetate discs and were deposited in the Library of Congress (catalog numbers AFS 19187–19219; preservation copies on reel-to-reel tape, catalog numbers 19038–19040). The collection includes two songs honoring Chauncey Yellow Robe, one of which was sung by Luther Standing Bear. Judith Gray, Reference Specialist, American Folklife Center, Library of Congress, letter to author, January 23, 2003.

13. When I applied to the graduate program at New York University, Rosebud gave her blessing to my project by writing a letter of recommendation: "I have known Marjorie Weinberg for over thirty-five years. During that period of time, she has become a member of our family in a unique position of daughter, sister, aunt to the various members of our family. . . . In short, she has entrée to the Yellow Robe and White Horse families that no anthropologist would ever have because we consider her one of the family. We will be glad to help her in her further studies in any way we may."

14. Sharon Monahan, *New York Times*, July 31, 1983.

15. Barbara Goldstein Paltrow, *New York Times*, August 28, 1983.

16. Marjorie Weinberg, *New York Times*, August 28, 1983.

17. Rosebud Yellow Robe, *New York Times*, September 18, 1983.

18. For example, one 320-acre chunk of rolling, grassy hills on the reservation has 450 owners. Some own pieces smaller than a newspaper. Under the federal laws that govern Indian tribes, each owner holds an "undivided interest." To do anything on this land, the owner needs the consent of all the other owners. This problem is called "fractionation."

19. Moses, a retired U.S. Army general, was not Indian but had been raised on the Rosebud Reservation. He died in the fall of 2000 and was buried with highest military honors at Arlington National Cemetery; I attended his funeral.

20. Personal correspondence, Emogene Paulson to the author, 1991.

21. The museum, founded in 1883, was named for William H. Over, one of its early directors, and continues his work of researching the heritage of South Dakota. Located on the university campus, its current building houses the state's largest collection of natural and cultural history.

22. The Clarks were missionaries on the Crow Creek Reservation, South Dakota.

23. In 1992, in Rosebud's name, I established a scholarship for Indian women at the University of South Dakota.

24. After my twin sons were born on Rosebud's birthday, the celebration of that day became the social event of our year.

25. On each anniversary of Rosebud's birthday, a notice appears in *New York Times*: "To the wind beneath our wings, with our love to Rosebud from your birthday club."

26. The invitation was extended by Karen Blu, my graduate adviser and friend.

27. At the end of Canon Ed's stay in the United States I wanted to find some special way to repay him for his guidance. When he said there was nothing he could accept but our thanks, I replied, "Okay, Canon, but I will come to Ireland, take you and your family out to dinner, and tell them how wonderful you've been to Rosebud and me." Soon after Rosebud's death the opportunity arose, and I was on my way to Ireland to repay a debt of the heart. Completing the circle with gifts for Ed's children and with a special dinner, I tried to express our heartfelt gratitude for the consolation he had brought to Rosebud and me.

28. A published version appears in E. Wendell Lamb and Lawrence W. Schultz, *Indian Lore* (Winona Lake, IN: Light and Life Press, 1964).

29. Ann needed a model for a life-size portrait representing a Seminole Indian woman, commissioned by the Historical Museum of Southern Florida in Miami. She also painted two other life-size portraits of Rosebud in Lakota dress, one of

which is in the collections of the W. H. Over Museum at the University of South Dakota, and the other in my home in Santa Fe.

EPILOGUE

1. That year, in Rosebud's name, I established a scholarship at Sinte Gleska University to aid Indian women.

2. My husband and I visited with Deb on several occasions over the next few years, but in 1999 she died at the age of forty-five from complications of lupus. We returned for memorial services and a powwow honoring her memory. She had been a remarkable young woman, well known and respected throughout South Dakota. Most important for me, she had become a supportive and dear friend. A professional therapist for the Department of Corrections, she was also a sought-after singer for rodeos, powwows, and church programs. She served on the board of directors of the Crazy Horse Memorial, the monumental sculpture being carved on a mountain in the Black Hills near Custer, South Dakota, and always sang at the public events held there. She was frequently interviewed by national print and broadcast media concerning the memorial. She expressed pride in it: "I believe the sculpture can change people's hearts. As they begin to find out about Crazy Horse, they begin to seek knowledge not only about him but the culture that bore him. When they reach out to that culture, they reach out to us" (*Crazy Horse Progress,* September 6, 1999, publication of the Crazy Horse Memorial Foundation).

3. *National Dance Institute Newsletter,* spring 1994.

4. The project also involved an extensive pen-pal network by which students from around the world, including some American Indian communities, corresponded with one another.

5. *Rosebud's Song* was performed again on May 23.

6. It was my privilege to donate the plaque, not only to commemorate Rosebud's achievements but, more important, to introduce her to the current generation of visitors so that they too would know about this part of Jones Beach history.

References

Arnold, Elliott. *Blood Brother*. New York: Duell, Sloan & Pearce, 1947.

Bordewich, Fergus M. *Killing the White Man's Indian: Reinventing Native Americans at the End of the Twentieth Century*. New York: Doubleday, 1996.

Bronson, Ruth Muskrat. *Indians Are People, Too*. New York: Friendship Press, 1947.

Brown, Ruth. Biography of Chauncey Yellow Robe. Unpublished manuscript, 1929. Rosebud Yellow Robe Family Papers, privately held; copy in the author's possession.

Castle, Edward. "Rosebud: Solution to Mystery Offered; Tattered CBS Radio Ledger Tells Tale of 'Rosebud' Roots," *Las Vegas Sun*, August 11, 1991, 1A.

Cohen, Lucy. "Swift Bear Winter Count." *Indians at Work*, January 1942, p. 14, and February 1942, p. 30.

Coordinating Committee on American Indian Affairs. "Minutes of Meeting, Coordinating Committee on American Indian Affairs, October 20, 1948." Typescript, Mary Cabot Wheelwright Collection, Wheelwright Museum of the American Indian, Santa Fe NM.

Crazy Horse Progress. September 6, 1999. Crazy Horse, SD: Crazy Horse Memorial Foundation.

Deloria, Ella C. *Speaking of Indians*. New York: Friendship Press, 1944.

Fielder, Mildred. *Sioux Indian Leaders*. Seattle WA: Superior, 1975.

Gray, John S. *Centennial Campaign: The Sioux War of 1876*. Norman: University of Oklahoma Press, 1988.

Gridley, Marion, ed. and comp. *Indians of Today*. Sponsored by the Indian Council Fire. Chicago: Millar, 1947.

Grutman, Jewel H. *The Ledgerbook of Thomas Blue Eagle*. Atlanta GA: Lickle, 1994.

A History of Pennington County, South Dakota. N.p., n.d. (c. 1985).

Hyde, George E. *Spotted Tail's Folk: A History of the Brulé Sioux*. Norman: University of Oklahoma Press, 1961.

Lamb, Thomas G. *Eight Bears: A Biography of E. W. Deming, 1860–1942*. Oklahoma City OK: Griffith Books, 1978.

Lamb, E. Wendell, and Lawrence W. Schultz. *Indian Lore*. Winona Lake IN: Light and Life Press, 1964.

McBride, Bunny. *Molly Spotted Elk: A Penobscot in Paris*. Norman: University of Oklahoma Press, 1995.

O'Harra, C. C. "President Coolidge in the Black Hills." *Black Hills Engineer*, November 1927.

Olson, James C. *Red Cloud and the Sioux Problem*. Lincoln: University of Nebraska Press, 1965.

Powers, Mabel (Yehsennohwehs). *Around an Iroquois Camp Fire*. New York: Frederick A. Stokes, 1923.

———. *Stories the Iroquois Tell Their Children*. New York: American Book Company, 1917.

Pratt, Richard H. *The Indian Industrial School, Carlisle, Pennsylvania* (1908). Introduction by Robert M. Utley. Carlisle PA: Cumberland County Historical Society, 1979.

———. Manuscript collection. Beinecke Library, Yale University, New Haven CT.

Riney, Scott. *The Rapid City Indian School, 1898–1933*. Norman: University of Oklahoma Press, 1999.

Smith, Donald B. *Chief Buffalo Child Long Lance: The Glorious Impostor*. Red Deer AB, Canada: Red Deer Press, 1999.

Society of American Indians. *Proceedings of the Fourth Annual Conference of the Society of American Indians*. Madison WI: Society of American Indians, 1914.

Sprenger, Hulda, and Meta Sprenger. *On the Trail of the Sprengers*. Winterthur, Switzerland: Privately published, 2000.

Springer, Lillian Belle. Correspondence, 1905–27. In the possession of the author.

Standing Bear, Luther. *My People the Sioux*. Boston: Houghton Mifflin, 1928.

Thomson, David. *Rosebud: The Story of Orson Welles*. New York: Alfred A. Knopf, 1996.

Walker, James R. *Lakota Belief and Ritual*. Ed. Raymond J. DeMallie and Elaine A. Jahner. Lincoln: University of Nebraska Press, 1980.

Weinberg, Marjorie. "Rosebud Yellow Robe and the Jones Beach Indian Village." Master's thesis, New York University, 1990.

Wheeler, Robert W. *Jim Thorpe: World's Greatest Athlete*. Norman: University of Oklahoma Press, 1988.

Whitehorn, Chester. "Her Name Is Rosebud." *Cue* (Long Island edition), May 5, 1951.

White Horse, Chauncina. "The Indians of Chicago: A Perspective." In *Urban Indians: Proceedings of the Third Annual Conference on Problems and Issues concerning American Indians Today*, pp. 78–81, Occasional Papers Series 4. (Chicago: Newberry Library Center for the History of the American Indian, 1981).

Williams, Jack R. "The Greatest Bonnet Maker of Them All!" *American Indian Hobbyist* 4, nos. 7–8 (1958): 64–65.

Yellow Robe, Chauncey. "My Boyhood Days." *Indian Leader*, October 30, 1925. Reprinted as "Grand-Nephew of 'Sitting Bull' Is a Leading Educator," *American Indian*, December 1926, 5, 12.

Yellow Robe, Richard (Search the Enemy). "An Indian Boy's Experience." *Indian Helper* 3, no. 17 (1887).

Yellow Robe, Rosebud. *An Album of the American Indian*. New York: Franklin Watts, 1969.

———. Preface to Elaine Mei Aoki et al., *Write Idea!* New York: Macmillan/Mc-Graw-Hill School Publishing, 1993.

———. *Tonweya and the Eagles*. New York: Dial Books for Young Readers, 1979.

Index